GEORGE E. GOERIG

R.S.V.P. CHINA

R.S.V.P. China

For information about this title or to order other books and/or electronic media, contact the publisher:

ACG Press
Web: DoctorAce.com

ISBN: 979-8-9880408-4-2 (softcover)
ISBN: 979-8-9880408-5-9 (eBook)

Printed in the United States of America

Cover and interior design: 1106 Design

CHAPTER 1

The continuous streaks of lightning that suddenly began to flash over the tangled foliage of the jungle that mainly comprised the desolate country known as Burma were closely followed by breathtaking claps of thunder. As the warm raindrops began to drum off his steel helmet, George automatically shook his head. Silently, he muttered to himself, "What am I doing out here in this God-forsaken land, and what the hell is going to happen next?"

Grudgingly, he approved of the natural reflexes that sent his motley crew of Nepalese laborers scurrying over to the two canvas-covered British lorries parked on the side of the Ledo Road. Taking advantage of the sudden drastic change of weather, the private, who had been unfortunately demoted from his rank of buck sergeant the previous week, purposely walked over to the hastily built, temporary lean-to he hoped would provide at least meager shelter from the downpour he knew was inevitable.

Cautiously sitting down on the crude, improvised stool he had made, George mumbled to himself, "At least those dumb, lazy foreign bastards know when it's time to get in out of the rain."

Again, another resounding roar from the darkened skies caused Goerig to draw his supposedly rainproof GI coat closer around himself. As he sat hunched over, perspiring and bracing himself against the driving sheets of rain, the private began to reflect on the unfortunate happenings of the past couple of weeks that had placed him in his precarious position.

The sad fact that his construction battalion had been performing at only half its potential really should have been no worry of his. Then came the day the inspector general stopped by and inquired about the company's efficiency. That was when he opened his big mouth.

"Yes sir, we would like to have a change of officers in the organization. With competent supervisory personnel, I am sure we could increase our efficiency by at least 50 percent."

The officer had been very attentive and expressed his desire to look into the matter. However, he had been committed at the time to continue on up to Mychtina where Merrill's Marauders had just cleaned out the Japs. He did suggest, though, that a list of concrete complaints be drawn up and that the men agreeing should sign the petition and send it down to his office.

George had been amazed. "But sir, such a petition during a period of war is a general court martial offense. That I can do without."

When the inspector general had convinced him that under the circumstances everything would be all right, the sergeant had boldly proceeded to do as the officer had suggested, much to his own sorrow. Five days after their meeting, George was informed that the inspector general had died of a heart attack up in Mychtina. He stared vacantly out at the forbidding jungle and wondered, "What's coming next?"

Without warning, the roar of a jeep's engine brought the private slowly to his feet. He watched anxiously as the mud-splattered vehicle recklessly rounded a corner of the rutted road and splashed to a screeching halt in front of him.

"George, get your fanny in here and get the hell out of the rain. I've got some news for you."

Immediately, the bewildered private recognized the tired, grim features of Pat Doyle, the sergeant major who was the top non-com for the battalion.

"What's up, Sarge?" George expectantly asked as he slid over the sodden, canvas-covered seat next to his unexpected visitor.

The answer came promptly. "First of all, here's a letter from one Captain Jack Ferdon of the G2 Intelligence Office down in Calcutta. Perhaps you had better read that first. Is he a friend of yours?"

The private hastily tore open the envelope and scanned the short note. "Keep your nose clean. Play it cool and stay out of any future trouble. You have just been exonerated from your potential court martial. Best regards, Jack."

George's first reactions were that of astonishment and confusion as he reflected back to his civilian days when he had made the acquaintance of a very congenial young lieutenant who was visiting mutual friends at the Lakeside Courts on the shores of Lake Washington where he lived. During his brief stay in the Northwest, Jack had been a pleasant addition to the numerous parties that were a common occurrence at that time. Hence, the latter's presence in the China-Burma-India theater of war came as a complete and welcoming surprise.

Ignoring the eager, questioning glance on the sergeant's face, George quickly stuffed the warning message into a pocket of his oversized raincoat. With a forced smile and meanwhile expecting the worst, the private hesitantly ventured, "Okay now, what else?"

Without answering, Doyle reached back and pulled out a leather brief case from the rear seat. Opening it up, he carefully withdrew an official-looking piece of paper. Cautiously protecting it from the rain, the sergeant major smilingly replied, "George, you happen to be a very fortunate young man at this time. Here is our answer to a formal RSVP letter from China. General Chennault of the Fourteenth Air Force, previously the Flying Tigers, requested that three men, based on civilian qualifications, be transferred to China in order to supervise the construction of some airbases over there. Realizing your dire predicament about that possible court martial coming up, I managed to convince the colonel that you were the logical and most capable man for the job. It's all been okayed at headquarters, and you should be on your way in a few days or so. How do you like those apples?"

The disbelieving expression on Goerig's face suddenly changed to one of bewildered astonishment as he thought to himself, "Thank God, no court martial and a transfer out of this hell hole. This is the answer to my prayers."

As the relentless rain began to pour down in earnest, George instinctively pulled the collar of his coat closer around his neck and quizzically hollered over the impatient roar of the jeep's revved-up motor. "Just for the helluva it, Pat, it might sound stupid, but I guess I've forgotten. What does RSVP actually stand for?"

Doyle glanced at the quizzical private skeptically and then patiently began to explain as another furious clap of thunder seemed to shake the entire jungle around them.

"Who the hell cares?" he yelled. "You're getting out of this damned outfit. That's the main thing. However, since you want to know, the phrase comes from the French. As I recall from high school, it goes something like 'repondez s'il vous plait,' which means, 'We are expecting an answer.' Does that sound right to you?"

George contentedly leaned back as the increasingly angry storm buffeted the small vehicle. Completely oblivious to his surroundings, he slowly murmured the golden words to himself, "RSVP China—here I come."

CHAPTER 2

The year was nineteen hundred and forty-three. Franklin Delano Roosevelt was the president and the commander-in-chief of the United States Armed Forces. At this time his country was critically involved in a massive war with the Axis Powers, Germany and Japan.

George Goerig, the author of this incredulous story, was a contented civilian at the time. He was also managing to bear up with all the so-called hardships the civilian population had to endure during those trying months. The natural acceptance of the normal necessities of life had been seriously threatened by the introduction of a new trend in everyone's social life. It was called the ration book.

Actually, the situation was not too bad. The fact that the alcoholic content had been increased in imported rum seemed to partially satisfy the insatiable thirst of the millions determined to escape from reality for a little while one way or another.

There were various other inane melodies that aimed at easing people's worries about the tragic events unfolding around the world. It was a time when the famous crooners Crosby, Columbo, and Vallee were being overtaken in the popularity polls by a young, skinny, unknown singer who had worked for Harry James and Tommy Dorsey. His name was Frank Sinatra.

Goerig remembered him well. His famous voice, which made teenage girls swoon, was coming out over the radio as George entered the small apartment on that unforgettable night in August. Helen, his wife, had met him at the door, and after an exceptionally tender kiss, reluctantly handed him an official-looking piece of paper. It was from the president. It began simply with "Greetings."

George had been very fortunate up to that point in managing to avoid the draft. Construction of air bases were a vital part in the country's defense plans. It was especially so in the vast unprotected area around the vulnerable Boeing plant in Seattle, Washington, which was producing the famous B-17, better known as the Flying Fortress.

Prior to that eventful day in August, Goerig had been in the employment of his brother's construction business as a general superintendent. At the time his activities were centered on the building of an important military air base known by the Indian name of Kitsap. It was located near Bremerton, across Puget Sound from Seattle, his hometown.

His marriage to Helen could still be classified as being in the newlywed stage, even though they were the proud parents of a baby boy. Their residence was a small apartment in a complex of sixteen units, primarily occupied by young couples and their new offspring. Its name was Lakeside Court, or more aptly known as Fertile Valley.

Located on the shores of the inviting blue green waters of Lake Washington, the surrounding landscape was dominated by the majestic, snow-covered peak of Mount Rainier, which prevailed over the entire countryside.

The formidable range of the nearby Cascade mountains presented another awesome view, which provided a spectacular background to the land they called God's country.

Now, against his wishes, Goerig was going to have to leave all of this for a strange and questionable future in the Armed Forces. Destination unknown. He had previously applied for a commission at the start of the war but had been rejected on the grounds that one of his eyes failed to pass the twenty-twenty vision requirement. His college degree had been no help to him at the time, nor had the many years of experience in the construction field. In view of this, he figured that as long as he was going to retain his civilian status, it might as well be in a role where he could be at least useful to the war effort.

However, George learned that there still was a possibility of receiving a direct commission in the construction branch of the Army Corps of Engineering. With this in mind, he contacted his induction officer. There he was politely informed that in order to receive a direct commission, an applicant would have to be at least twenty-eight years of age. Unfortunately, George was only twenty-six.

Noting the obvious disappointment on the the young man's face, the recruiting captain helpfully suggested that he request to enlist as a private in an engineering branch of the Army, and after three months of basic training, he would be eligible to apply for a commission as a second lieutenant. However, the officer stipulated that he would have to obtain his commanding officer's approval.

It sounded great to the civilian, and what the hell was three months? If he had only known.

═

THE MEMORIES OF HIS FIRST unforgettable night at the Fort Lewis Indoctrination Center, just south of Seattle, were very vivid in Goerig's mind. He couldn't help but recall the realistic and familiar phrase that seemed very appropriate at the time: "There is no place like home."

After a week of being processed and going through the military routine of indoctrination, including inoculations, physical drills, inspections, and the like, Private Goerig was treated, free of charge, to a very interesting movie. It had something to do with sex and stressed the dire results of contacting gonorrhea or syphilis. With this important educational background, he was prepared to move on to his nest destination, Geiger Field in Spokane, Washington. Fortunately, it was Helen's hometown, and she was able to move in with her mother, who resided there.

═

It didn't take George very long to realize that he didn't relish the idea of being a private in the Army for the duration of the war; no one wants to be a private.

With this in mind, he decided that at the first opportunity he would ask for an audience with his commanding officer, Lieutenant Paine. At this time, however, Private Goerig had no way of knowing that the lieutenant was going to become such an important factor in his military future. Actually, the most appropriate word was to be nemesis.

After a dutiful salute and standing at the best at-attention stance he knew at the time, George preceded to inform his superior of the previous discussion he had had with his induction officer in regard to a possible future commission following his three months of basic training. The lieutenant seemed rather impressed with Goerig's past educational background and his construction experience. He had politely allowed the private the allocated time he spared for new recruits and finally told him he would keep the request in mind. With this to look forward to, George dutifully saluted and left the office.

═

FORTUNATELY, THE THREE MONTHS of basic training seemed to pass quickly, despite the arduous twenty-mile hikes with full packs and the resultant painful blisters. Following this period of physical training and the pertinent education on what to do in case of chemical warfare, the anxious recruit was finally given permission to go over to Seattle and obtain the necessary papers for his promised commission. The induction officer was true to his word.

"All you have to do now, George, is to get your CO's signature on these papers and you'll be on your way to become a commissioned officer. Good luck."

Goerig hastened back to Geiger Field and confidently presented the required request to Lieutenant Paine. Reluctantly, the officer said he would go over the papers and notify the private when the request had been properly processed and approved. In the meantime, in a placating manner, he told George that he had been recommended for sergeant's stripes. The latter immediately sensed that the lieutenant had no intention of approving the request for an advancement to the status of a commissioned officer for this enlisted man. However, Goerig did thank his CO for the advancement in rank, dutifully saluted, and left sad.

A few days had passed by when he was finally notified to report to the company headquarters. As he nervously stood at attention in front of his superior's desk, George listened incredulously as the former soap salesman dealt him a final crushing blow that left him in a complete daze.

"Tough shit, Goerig. The battalion has been alerted to go overseas. You are going with us, so you might as well forget about that commission you thought you were going to get. That's the way the cookie crumbles. You are dismissed."

As the crisp, arrogant words slowly began to penetrate his numbed brain, George automatically saluted, turned, and quickly strode through the open doorway to the outer office. Pausing momentarily by the first sergeant's desk, he angrily muttered, "Someday, somewhere, I am going to get even with that double-crossing son of a bitch. I just got a good screwing."

CHAPTER THREE

It was a beautiful haven for sand dune lovers. It was vast, desolate, and very hot. Goerig had never appreciated the wonderful, green, timbered country of the great Northwest more than when the separate battalion was temporarily bivouacked a few miles from the New Mexico town of Alamogordo. They were finally on their way overseas.

It was April 1944 and the eagerness of the newly formed group to be an active participant in the far-off war was prominently displayed in the rapid construction of a temporary tent camp and an adjacent airfield. The men were finally doing their thing and seemed to enjoy it.

Fortunately, Helen was able to come down for a few days and her presence helped alleviate the loneliness of her husband's situation. She had obtained a room in one of the dilapidated hotels in the town. She also managed to survive one frightening night when an unexpected visitor attempted to open her door via the transom. Helen was not normally the screaming type, but George was to learn later that his wife's cries of alarm had awakened most of the sleeping tenants. Her uninvited visitor beat a hasty retreat.

Nine months later, pleasant tidings of a new arrival in the family made George appreciate the fact that Helen's visit was not completely in vain.

After two arduous weeks of adjusting themselves for the future construction work that lay ahead, the battalion was notified to pack up their

George and wife Helen.

gear and start moving. The tedious train trip to the East Coast was interesting despite the overcrowding. At least it eliminated conjectures about being headed to the Pacific Theater, unless somebody had "snafued" as they did later on.

Following a brief layover at Norfolk, Virginia, they boarded a troop ship and found themselves crammed into a tight space designed for efficiency, not comfort. After all, there was a war going on. After an uneventful trip across the Atlantic Ocean, the novice seafarers watched as their liner approached the Port of Oran, Africa. Goerig had always wished that someday he would be able to visit this far away, fascinating continent, but not under war-time conditions. The fabulous stories of the adventurous, exciting animal hunting safaris he had read about still seemed far over the distant horizon.

As George and his friends roamed the narrow, littered streets of the foreign city, he marveled at the amazing miracles Hollywood created starring Charles Boyer and Hedy Lamar, Humphrey Bogart and Ingrid Bergman, all doing their thing in God-forsaken hell holes such as these. A mattress cover was the basic rate of exchange among the GIs and the clever little begging urchins who followed the Americans wherever they went. Cognac was the popular, expensive drink and if you didn't like that, there was always the watered down wine. However, it was literally speaking "the only port in a storm."

The battalion's stay was a short one, and before they began to learn the customs of the foreign populace, the men found themselves on a converted luxury liner whose "scuttlebutt" destination was India. However, when the convoy they were a part of began plowing its way across the blue-green waters of the Mediterranean and headed north past the boot of Italy, all aboard became slightly puzzled, then very apprehensive as the ship's anchor was dropped in the embattled harbor of Naples. The other transports hurriedly proceeded to tie up at the crowded piers and unload their battle-destined troops and cargo.

Goerig and the others realized that there was a war going on and that the Americans had just taken over Naples. Also, they were well aware that the actual combat area was not far away. But what the hell were they doing there? George had always considered himself to be a lover and not much of a fighter—much better as the former and quite lousy as the latter.

It wasn't long before one of the local pilot boats approached the patiently waiting transport. After many quizzical looks and hand gesturing by its occupants, the captain was finally notified he was in the wrong convoy. Shortly before dark, two escorting naval ships cautiously guided the errant transport out of the harbor and steered south back to the welcoming waters of the blue Mediterranean.

As the relieved passengers lined the ship's rails, they could look back and clearly discern the explosion of bombs around and over Naples. Needless to say, the soldiers were very thankful to be leaving the inhospitable area.

After crossing the Mediterranean Ocean, which many years previously was referred to as Caesar's Lake by the Romans, the misguided liner approached the fabled shores of Egypt, the Land of the Pharaohs and the strategic Suez Canal. Slowly moving through the placid, narrow channel brought back memories of the popular movie *Suez* starring the handsome, popular Tyrone Power and the beautiful Annabella.

Passing the ancient monumental sights, like the Pyramids, of Egyptian history, created thousands of years before Christ, produced a very deep, sobering effect. At least Goerig was living his long-standing dream of such a trip. The war itself, at the time, was a far-gone reality.

Reaching India, the battalion disembarked at the Port of Bombay. They immediately became aware that the ravages of war had not passed over this fabulous city and its surrounding areas. The men were afforded a firsthand view of one of the greatest disasters of World War II. They boarded their troop train just before dusk, and soon after they pulled out of the station, the train entered a vast expanse of blackened shambles. On both sides was complete destruction for block after block. The factories between the railroad and the harbor were no more than skeletons of twisted steel. Beyond lay the wreckage of ships in fantastic disorder, and behind the industrial section were row on row of shells of tenement houses, like victims of a bombing blitz. Never had they seen such mass destruction. They had heard sketchy accounts of the disaster, but none had visualized a catastrophe of such dimensions as this one. It was only until much later that the full story was released.

The disaster that occurred on April 14, 1944, had its inception in a fire aboard the 8,000-ton *Liberty*, a ship tied up at dock in the harbor. Swarms of coolies had been unloading her cargo of scrap metal, baled cotton, a large sum in gold bullion, and several hundred tons of TNT when fire interrupted their work. Apparently beginning in the cotton cargo, it made rapid headway against all efforts to fight it. The Bombay fire brigade labored valiantly, at the cost of the lives of the majority of them, to bring the fire under control. As the fire raged on unchecked, frantic preparations were made to tow the ton of TNT into a less critical anchorage.

At four in the afternoon, the smoke changed from a brown smudge to a milky cloud, and a shaft of orange flame shot high in the air. A few minutes later, the ship exploded, spreading havoc in every direction. A 4,000-ton ship moored nearby was boosted, with broken back, onto a wharf. Another tossed her anchor into a neighbor's rigging. Destruction reigned.

A mile and more away, windows in the homes were shattered, and at lesser distances, fires sprang up in terrifying profusion. The city was substantially without a fire department, the greater part of the men and equipment having been on the dock. Smoke turned the afternoon into night. Fire, falling walls, and fear of the unknown created panic.

Police and troops were summoned hastily to carry on rescue work and combat the flames that threatened to engulf the city. For five days, US, British, and Indian troops fought the holocausts.

In the end, the official count stood at 360 dead, 1,815 injured, though the actual toll would never be known. Body parts floated in the harbor, representing uncounted casualties. Insurance claims were estimated at 150 million dollars, actual losses being much higher, and at least 50,000 were homeless.

There are no geographical boundaries for the victims of modern warfare.

The tedious train trip across the poverty-stricken land of India was one that a self-respecting hobo back in the States would have politely declined. The so-called "passenger" cars were ancient, outmoded, small, and definitely not even third class. However, since it was the only means of transportation to their eventual destination, the men grudgingly accepted the fact and made the best of the situation.

Hundreds of starving, shriveled-up specters of human beings surrounded the cars at every stop. It was a pitiful and deplorable sight.

Troops

By this time, the weary train travelers were fairly certain of where they were going—Burma. Their speculation as to why they were designated for that desolate outpost of civilization was a minor matter, but it did make for casual conversation. The fact that they were not headed for an actual combat area was something that they could definitely be thankful for.

For several hot, humid days and nights, the panorama of India slipped by. The men had not eluded the incessant heat that had engulfed them in the Suez Canal. The water situation was deplorable. Tanks above the several lavatories had remained empty for long periods, making sanitation a problem. For drinking water, the battalion had chlorinated their own in large jugs that had been bought from native vendors.

Finally, the steaming train reached Calcutta, its final destination. The fabulous and intriguing stories Goerig had read about this mysterious city were brought back to mind. While under early British rule, it had been referred to by the English as "The Black Hole of India." It had been the scene of many rebellions and bloody skirmishes between the Indian natives and soldiers from the British Isles.

The majority of the men were disappointed that their stay was very brief, for it was not long until they were again on the move.

The next adventurous portion of the interesting and educational trip was a boat ride up the Brahmaputra River. The mode of transportation was an ancient sternwheeler built in 1897. Without incident, it brought the battalion closer to its eventual objective, Ledo.

CHAPTER FOUR

Ledo, the construction equipment assembly depot for the building of the Burma Road in the China, Burma, India theater of war, was a welcome sight for the weary travelers. However, even there the normal amount of organized confusion was apparent. It took several days before headquarters decided where the five companies comprising Goerig's battalion were going to be located.

The Burma Road, as it was wore commonly known in most sectors, was at this stage a glorified jungle trail. Its importance consisted in eventually becoming a lifeline of military supplies to nationalist China in its crucial battle against the forces of the Japanese Imperial Army.

Finally, Goerig's company soon found itself encamped at a leach-infested location in the middle of a very dense and forbidding jungle not too many miles from Ledo, the starting point. Their new, green-painted heavy construction equipment had arrived, and the men were anxious to begin the task of clearing, grading, and graveling the portion of the future primitive highway that had been assigned to them.

At this point, the prospect of finally realizing he was going to be aiding in the war effort, even in a minimal way, made Goerig very enthusiastic. He was happy to be there. His duties consisted in supervising the installation of the essential galvanized stool culverts that were an important factor in the rain-plagued country.

As work progressed, the knowledgeable operators and construction men worked in harmony with the young, inexperienced soldiers to show them the proper techniques used in building roads. Things looked great at the start. However, after a few weeks, it became quite apparent that something was wrong.

The necessary planning ahead and essential "follow up," which were common construction procedures, were sadly missing. The lack of overall necessary organization and direction became very obvious to several of the older, more experienced men. It began to express itself in the eventual confusion.

After several impromptu meetings with the other disillusioned former civilian "hardhats," Goerig came to the conclusion that something had to be done to rectify the situation. The fact that he felt he had been unjustly deprived of the commission by his commanding officer had no bearing on his feelings at that late time. He was waiting for the right opportunity to personally express his views and those of others who sided with him. It was not long in coming.

The unexpected meeting occurred on one hot and sultry afternoon as George was busily burning the leaches off his legs with a cigarette. The blood-sucking parasites seemed to be able to crawl onto any area of a person's body after they had inadvertently been brushed off the green jungle foliage. The sergeant didn't smoke, but he soon discovered that a lighted cigarette was practically the only device for removing the little blood hungry bastards. So naturally, after twenty-seven years he began smoking. It was one minor vice he had managed to escape, up to that time.

Suddenly, a dust-covered jeep noisily drove up and pulled over to the side of the road. A fairly tall, huskily built man stepped out and, after stretching his legs, walked over to Goerig. He had a friendly, disarming smile on his perspiring face as he reached out to shake the enlisted man's hand.

"Sergeant Goerig, I presume?"

George felt like quipping that he definitely was not Doctor Livingston but wisely refrained.

"Yes sir, what can I do for you?"

The officer continued. "My name is Major Harrison, and I am with the inspector general's office. After talking with several of your friends down the road, they referred me to you in regard to any complaints you might have. If you wish to discuss them with me, I would be only too glad to hear them."

Goerig hesitated for a moment while he pondered whether he was being "duped" or if the major was actually leveling with him. He decided on the latter.

"Major," the sergeant began, "I could name innumerable incidents and situations that arise every day that, in my mind—and due to lack of proper overall supervision and organization—have definitely affected the morale and efficiency of the entire company."

"What would you suggest?" the officer politely asked.

With renewed, confidence, Goerig carried on. "I believe that a change in our leadership is essential. With suitable, qualified men in charge, I know there would be a terrific improvement in the time it will take to complete this section of road. In addition, I am sure the attitude of the men would be vastly improved." Hesitatingly, George paused and then looked up to the major questioningly. "Whether or not such competent officers are available, I don't know. However, if I had several hours to get together with two other sergeants in the outfit, I am sure we could present our side of this situation to your satisfaction."

Major Harrison glanced at the enlisted man skeptically and seemed to be weighing the matter in his mind before he spoke. Finally, he offered, "Sergeant, I am deeply interested in what you have said and also in the comments of some of the other men. However, at the present time, I have urgent business up at Myitkyina. Merrill's Marauders have finally got a toehold on the Japs, and we have taken over a large portion of territory there. I am not sure how long I will be detained. But I do have a suggestion—why not get together with your two other sergeant friends and make out a list of your concrete complaints that seem to be affecting the efficiency of your company? Nothing petty, however. Have the men, who comply with the complaints, sign the paper. Your commanding officer can then send it down to my office in Ledo. Upon, I hope, my return by plane, I assure you that some corrective action will be taken on your behalf. That is my job."

George's sudden, puzzled expression caused the officer to pause.

"But sir, that would be a petition, and I understand that a petition during war time calls for an automatic general court martial."

"I realize that," confirmed the major. "However, there are circumstances that can be taken into consideration. I believe such circumstances exist here. With my limited time and the fact that this matter will be handeled solely through my office, I don't believe you will have anything to worry about. George, I wish you the best of luck."

With a wave of his hand, the major climbed back in the jeep with his enlisted aide at the wheel and quickly departed in a cloud of dust.

Goerig momentarily reflected upon their brief conversation and muttered to himself, "Well, dammit, maybe things will get better. What do we have to lose? Not our necks, I hope."

George wasted no time in locating his sergeant friends, Gordon and Doyle. He related his conversation with the major and was quickly assured of their support. In order to ensure their privacy, they went over to the office of the USO representative. Swearing her to secrecy, the trio began the exacting task of listing only those complaints they deemed important enough to warrant the attention of Major Harrison. After several hours, the sergeants had compiled approximately thirty complaints. They also added suggestions to remedy the same. At the head of the paper was Captain Paine's replacement, and at the head of the list of prospective petitioners was Goerig's name followed closely by those of Gordon and Doyle. The difficult part of the project was yet to come.

Reaching all the men in the company was not an easy task. The soldiers were well spread out over the six miles of road, performing their duties in regard to the various phases of construction. However, their Yankee ingenuity came through. Without the knowledge of the officers, various messengers carrying out their official duties were able to disperse copies of the petition throughout the company. Ninety-five percent of the enlisted men affixed their signature to the underground document. The remaining 5 percent were considered a dubious minority who might have gladly revealed the project to their superiors in order to curry the latter's favor.

Upon the completion of this portion of their plan, Steve Gordon was elected to take the completed requests down to the inspector general's office in Ledo. Using some implausible excuse, the sergeant managed to hitch a ride to the main base and personally deliver the papers to Major Harrison's enlisted secretary. After he returned the next day, the trio figured all they could do was wait. It wasn't long.

Doctor McAvoy was the medical officer for the battalion. Coincidently, he had been a fellow resident with George and Helen at Fertile Valley back in Seattle. They had formed a close friendship, and it had been a pleasant surprise when Goerig had found out earlier that the captain was also a member of the battalion. He had made few trips up the road to his section; hence the sergeant was mildly surprised when the officer's jeep drew up alongside of him on the road. It was about a week following Sergeant Gordon's return.

McAvoy jumped out of the still-running jeep and hurried over. "George, what the hell have you done?" he shouted.

Figuring his past activities might be what his friend was excited about, Goerig tried to calm him down while he explained what had happened. All his illegal actions had been condoned by the inspector general, and they were just waiting his return from Myitkyina.

"George, the inspector general had a heart attack in Myitkyina, and he died three days ago," the doctor sadly announced.

When Goerig finally recovered from the unexpected news, he hesitantly inquired. "What about the petition?"

He immediately sensed a feeling of pity come over the captain.

"Right now, it is in the battalion headquarters office. It seems that it was forwarded to General Peck following the death of Major Harrison. He subsequently called in our colonel and, from what I hear, all hell broke loose.

The colonel is headed up here now, and your Captain Paine is due to be dragged over the coals. If he is still left in the driver's seat up here, you and your friends are in for a bad time."

With a feeble shrug of his shoulders, George meekly asked, "What now?" The private seemed resigned to an uncertain and foreboding future.

The doctor put his arm around George's shoulder. "Well, hang in there. If I can be of any help, I'll sure as hell try."

With this, he climbed back into his jeep, revved up the sputtering engine, and headed back to his headquarters in Ledo.

It was about four hours later when a company jeep passed Goerig as he was directing the installation of a culvert. Later, he noticed the same vehicle returning towards the campsite with Sergeants Gordon and Doyle in the rear seat. They both appeared very solemn and merely nodded their heads as they went by. George understandably figured that it wouldn't be long now.

Upon finishing his work for the day, Goerig hitched a ride on one of the gravel trucks and was soon back at his tent. After anxiously inquiring about the status of his two friends, he learned that they had been "shipped out" to Ledo.

As time went by, it eventually occurred to Goerig that perhaps Captain Paine had something special planned for him. It was apparent that his usually friendly buddies were not so friendly and that they were purposely avoiding him. At chow time, George tried to find out what had really happened during the day. Nobody seemed to actually know. However, there had been a lot of "brass" around the office, and it appeared that the petition might have had something to do with it. Realizing that there was nothing to gain by further inquiries, the sergeant had chow and went to bed. He did manage to get some sleep, but mostly it was a case of tossing and turning and wondering what was in store for him.

Work continued as usual on the road. It was about four days after the conversation with Captain McAvoy that Goerig was unceremoniously picked up at his job and hurriedly driven to the company's headquarter office. He was greeted by the first sergeant as the latter nodded his head toward the "inner sanctum." George entered and stood at attention as his superior thumbed through some papers he had in his hands. After a few awkward minutes, the captain looked up.

"Sergeant Goerig, you are now a private. You will take out a 'D' handle shovel tomorrow and work with the Indian laborers."

"Captain," Goerig replied, "I'll take out that 'D' handle shovel tomorrow, but I will not work with it."

"You will not *what?*"

"I will not work with it, SIR!"

"You realize what you have done?"

"Yes."

"Yes, what?"

"Yes SIR!"

With a wave of his hand, Paine turned back to his papers.

"You are dismissed."

George dutifully saluted and left a very red faced and very mad Captain Paine. As he passed the first sergeant, with whom he got along with fine, the latter gave him a feeble grin. The new private felt this was only the beginning. How right he was.

Life up to this point had not been too bad. Various types of jungle life occasionally showed themselves. Monkeys and their constant chattering created quite an interesting, noisy background. One day, in the leafy shelter of a tree, some soldiers found a small baby gorilla that had been deserted by its mother and they had taken it to camp. It provided amusement for the men who tried to feed and care for it. However, despite their efforts, the lonely ape shortly died and was given a proper burial.

Next, the soldiers found a small, baby leopard and brought it to camp. The constant problem of large rats that infested the camp was temporarily solved as the new pet was turned loose in the tent barracks. It was a typical cat-and-mouse game until the rats would get cornered and try to fight back. Then there would be a sudden flurry of spots and the game would be quickly over.

The men had been warned of the presence of various deadly snakes in the area and were always on the alert for them. One of the most feared was the King Cobra. The arrival of snakes in the camp site was announced by the sudden disappearance of the rats. The men learned to take the wise preventive measure of checking to see if one of the deadly snakes had wound itself around a man's boots during the night. This had to be done after waking in the morning before getting out of bed and reaching for one's shoes. Any sudden, unintentional disturbance could prove quite costly and possibly fatal.

One day, while working on the road, a group of the soldiers became fascinated by the weaving motions of a large cobra. They discreetly kept a safe distance. A small boy of the Naga head-hunting tribe walked unobtrusively out of the jungle and right up to the snake. With a quick flourish of his three-foot blade, he deftly lopped off the head of the menacing reptile and casually continued on his way. Most of the men felt rather sheepish about the incident but merely shrugged it off as an example of the fight for existence in the steaming jungle.

Adjacent to the company's section of road construction, a negro battalion was busily engaged in pushing forward on their designated portion of the road.

One day, Goerig had taken an opportunity to strike up a conversation with several of their members when one of them casually remarked, "Well, we got another CO today. I wonder how long he'll last. Somehow these 'whites' just don't dig this jungle life."

George immediately became interested and began questioning the black man regarding how many commanding officers they had had and how they were able to get them changed.

"Hell, man, we don't change them, we just got rid of them. It must be four or five by now. If we don't dig them, we just draw straws, and somebody eliminates the man."

Goerig's thoughts of a new solution to his company's problems vanished.

"What happens after you eliminate him?"

"Well, we figure one little old private is expendable and worth the price. Of course, he's got to be caught first and that won't be easy to do. But we're fair, we draw straws first."

Despite their seeming lack of fear of possible Army reprisals, the black soldiers did have a lot of respect for the men of the local Naga Indian tribe. *Respect*—that was putting it mildly. After discovering the cut-up remains of two of their buddies who had tried to engage in forbidden sexual relations with a Naga woman, the colored boys made a wide track around any approaching tribesmen. George thought, "Well, to each his own."

═

Goerig had previously read of the fabled, primitive Indian tribe of Upper Burma. The legend of the so-called Naga headhunters was true in one respect: they really did engage in headhunting. But their notorious activities in this regard were mostly limited to the intertribal warfare more common in earlier times. The prize of an enemy's decapitated head was a worthy symbol of a warrior's prowess.

Concerning their infrequent relations with the British or Americans, the Nagas had deep respect for the white man. During General Stillwell's forced "walkout" in the rainy month of May 1942 over the circuitous, mountain route that eventually led to India, it was this hospitable tribe that gratuitously aided him in his retreat in the face of the Japanese military forces. The proud Indians' deep respect for this great man was reflected in their contempt of any possible Nipponese reprisals for aiding in the general's withdrawal with the meager remnants of his forces.

The Nagas' villages lay nestled in the deep valleys between the formidable mountain ranges of Upper Burma. Their primary crops were rice, corn, and vegetables. It was the custom for generations that the old folks would see to it that the unmarried men and girls did all the work in the fields. As the story related, it seemed that the young bucks would much rather play around with the girls than work.

Most of the hill people would usually go naked when they labored amidst the crops. It saved on wearing out cloth, which was scarce and expensive. Hence the physical attractions of both boys and girls were on constant display.

After a while, the elders decided that the young bucks were taking too much time out to dally with the girls. That was bad for the harvest and meant the old men might have to go to work in order to increase the crop output. So, a few of the oldsters hit on a solution. It was called the Naga Ring and was created to ensure good behavior and a full day's labor.

It was an ingenious metal band that was snugly fitted over the young man's limp penis. When he got amorous ideas and his manhood began to swell, the resulting pain caused the erection to immediately subside. As a result, there was not much more he could do but work. If he ever attempted to take it off, he would be beaten unmercifully by the old men of the tribe.

Such was the customary order of social life among the Indians of Upper Burma. George reflected back on the romantic, adventurous tales of the American Indians he had read about when he was a boy. He briefly wondered if any of the famous tribal nations had ever attempted to discourage any of the sexually minded young braves with such devious methods concerning their premarital relations with the opposite sex.

He realized, however, that American historians were definitely limited in their censored, intimate descriptions regarding The Uninhibited Love Life of the American Indian Brave. Again, to each his own.

═

Finally, the long-awaited day arrived when George was summoned to report to the company headquarters. With bated breath, he stood briskly at attention before his nemesis, Captain Paine.

"Private, you are being transferred out of C-company. Consider yourself very lucky. Your records have been forwarded to the battalion headquarters in Ledo. There is a jeep waiting to take you down there. Now, pack your gawd-damn gear and get the hell out of my sight."

Goerig, not one who easily displayed his emotions, merely smiled at the expected announcement and smartly saluted.

"Thank you and goodbye."

"Goodbye, WHAT!"

"Goodbye, SIR!"

As the private happily left the headquarters shack, he swore to himself he would forget about the unfortunate past and think only of the future. "RSVP, China. Here I come."

CHAPTER FIVE

On October 4th, 1944, it was raining steadily in Chabua, India, a familiar sight not unusual for that locality and time of year. Goerig was enjoying his temporary leave while awaiting a flight out to Kunming, China, the next stop on his military agenda. He had been enjoying the third can of cool beer he had bought at the canteen in the recreation hall adjacent to the air base when he was approached by a curly haired young man.

"Hello, my name is Charlie Hindleman. I am a war correspondent from the *New York Times,* assigned to the CBI theater of war. Mind if I join you?"

The man's frank and cheerful attitude surprised the private as he rose and extended his hand. "Not at all. Sit down and be my guest. How about a can of beer? It really tastes quite good after several months' forced abstinence."

"No thanks," was the reply. "But I'll take a rain check on it. Had a fairly rough night with some of the fellows and I think I'd better coast for a while."

Then noticing George's barracks bag next to his chair, the reporter casually asked, "Coming or going?"

"Both," laughed Goerig. "Just came down off Ledo Road and hope to be in China tomorrow, weather permitting. You know much about what's going on over there?"

The correspondent sat down, leaned back in the black leather chair, and thoughtfully inhaled from the short, stemmed pipe he held in his hand. Then, carefully placing it on the table in front of him, he hesitantly began, "Well, yes and no. I just got in from Calcutta yesterday, myself. I happen to be headed in your direction also. However, according to some of the reports I've heard, it seems that the Japs are doing their damnedest to get to Kunming and cut off the supply route from India. If they manage to do that, it's going to be pretty rough on Chiang Kai-shek and his boys." The reporter paused and quizzically glanced at George. "How about yourself? Know where you're going?"

The enlisted man took another sip from his beer. "Not really. Supposed to be doing my small bit in helping to supervise the building of some air bases for General Chenault. Guess I'll find out more when I get to Kunming. Personally, I am more a lover than a fighter. I'm not really looking forward to any combat action. I'll leave that to the bigger fellows."

Hindleman laughed and then rose to his feet. "Well, I can see where I won't be able to get any 'scoop' from you, George. But I wish you the best of luck. Hope to see you around again some time."

The private stood up and put out his hand. "Maybe when this damn war is over. The sooner, the better. Enjoy yourself."

The correspondent turned and left as Goerig resumed his seat and continued sipping on his beer. He softly murmured to himself. "I'm not looking for any combat action but if it comes my way, I hope I'll be able to cope with it."

The weather surprisingly broke clear the next day, much to Goerig's pleasure. As the C-47 transport roared down the lengthened runway and then gracefully rose toward the blue, cloudless sky, George breathed a sigh of relief. At last, his RSVP China request was to become a reality.

The flight over The Hump with the awesome, breath-taking view of the lower, snow-covered Himalayan mountains gave the private a tingling thrill. However, he also shuddered at the remote chance of a possible forced landing on the treacherous, icy slopes.

Before boarding the plane, George had noticed several members of a volunteer USO group patiently awaiting their chance to get on the same transport for China. It was then that he recognized the familiar features of one of Hollywood's leading stars, Melvyn Douglas. The private was determined to find a seat close to the famous star so he might engage him in conversation. The opportunity presented itself when Goerig was able to slide onto one of the bucket seats directly across from the man who had made love to such actresses as Joan Crawford, Irene Dunne, and others.

As the transport continued its turbulent way, beset by occasional, perilous downdrafts of several hundred feet, Goerig leaned forward and hesitantly opened the conversation he had looked forward to.

"Mr. Douglas, my name is George Goerig. I am an ardent fan of yours. I would like to take this occasion to thank you for your volunteer work entertaining the GIs overseas. Also, if you don't mind, I would like to ask you a few personal questions about Hollywood and some of the actresses you have starred with."

The ruddy, flushed face of the renowned actor broke into his famous chuckle. "Thank you. I really enjoy these trips, and if I can bring any enjoyment to the troops, it is rewarding in itself." He paused and then continued. "About my associations with the famous actresses in Hollywood, you probably have read in the movie magazines more than I could ever tell you. However, don't believe everything you read. Fortunately, my record is clear, and I have had a very pleasurable time working with most of the screen actresses. Now, how about you? Where are you from and what are your future plans, without divulging any military secrets?"

Before George could relate his favorite story of when he had been a member of the University of Washington basketball team and they had visited the Warner Brothers' lot in Hollywood on their way to Hawaii, they were interrupted by an announcement from the co-pilot.

"Kunming next. Adjust your seat belts."

Kunming, black market city of China, headquarters of the Fourteenth Air Force, was the center of a tremendous influx of people because of the war. Thousands of homeless Chinese had moved to the terminus of the Burma Road and the Hump Air Route from the west. It was also the last stop on the refugee trail from the east.

George soon found himself temporarily stationed at one of the holding areas camps a few miles from the crowded city. While leisurely enjoying his delayed trip to Chungking, he took advantage of the various trips and entertainment supplied by the Red Cross personnel. In downtown Kunming, there was a four-story structure known as the American Building. It was the recreation center for the GIs located in the area and amply provided most of the entertainment for the homesick and morally conscious airmen. There were other modes of entertainment that could be enjoyed by unobtrusively visiting the sections which were posted as "Off Limits." The private was aware of these tempting so-called "dens of iniquity" but wisely refrained from visiting any of them.

Goerig also learned of the fact that his new Commanding General Clare Chennault had his main residence located in the upper-class section of the city. He had just recently married a young and beautiful Chinese girl who was a daughter of one of the leading families in China.

Finally, the long-awaited orders came through for the private to board another transport for Chungking. The uneventful trip to the acting capital of nationalist China ended after the C-47 had circled the devastated city, revealing the extensive bomb damage that had been wrought by the Japanese Air Force.

George had previously read, back in the States, of the many thousands of deaths caused by the indiscriminate destruction of the enemies' bombers, who had had little opposition. It was here that the Fourteenth Air Force Engineers had their headquarters.

Two other enlisted men, assigned to the same type of duty as himself, had accompanied Goerig on the flight. The three men were met at the airport and driven by jeep to the nearby airbase. It consisted of a mess hall and several wooden barracks plus a care-free group of young engineers whose main aim in life seemed to be centered around having an occasional party when time would allow. George was to find out later that such parties were a frequent occurrence.

It was at that time that Goerig met his future superior. His name was Captain Harold Lewis. George immediately took a liking to the man and silently marveled at the great disparity the Air Force was capable of when it came to their commissioned officers. He was stocky and short with a flushed, radiant face that seemed to indicate he was enjoying his work. The captain had a knack for making a person feel quite at ease, as he explained that he was not necessarily a military man. Previously, he had been associated with the City of New York Engineering Department. Briefly, he related to his new recruits what their future assignments would consist of.

The major involvement of their duties comprised the extension, widening, and resurfacing of three existing runways in the vicinity of the Hupeh Province of central China. The work was to be done by Chinese contractors, primarily from Chungking. It also would include the construction of essential buildings adjacent to the runways. Each enlisted man would be placed in charge of inspection with an interpreter to assist him. Captain Lewis would oversee all the sites and the trio would be directly responsible to him. It sounded too good to be true. Goerig silently thanked Pat Boyle back in Ledo and wondered if he could ever have the chance to repay him for this tremendous opportunity.

Taking advantage of the brief layover, the captain and George managed to indulge in a short snack at the mess hall before returning to the air terminal. Upon their arrival, George noticed the pilot of the waiting plane and a staff sergeant carrying on a heated argument.

"I'll never be able to get that damn plane off the ground!" shouted the pilot.

The sergeant retorted, "All equipment and personnel have been checked out and you are within the weight limits."

"For a new C-47, yes, but not that bucket of bolts," hollered the officer over the whining roar of the engines as they warmed up. "If you are so damn sure of yourself, why the hell don't you fly it? I'll stay here and go out to help pick up the pieces."

It was then that George noticed a couple of men quietly climb down from the plane with their barracks bags and head for the small terminal office.

"Where the hell do you think you're going?" roared the sergeant. "Get your ass back on that plane."

"Not if the captain doesn't think it's safe, we won't," was the rebellious answer.

At this point, the pilot threw up his hands resignedly. "Okay, climb back on the damn plane and we'll take a crack at it," he ordered.

Reluctantly, all the passengers boarded the aircraft as Goerig immediately noticed the cause of the discussion. Crated and displacing a large portion of the bare storage area in the transport was a fairly good sliced radio transmitter designated for one of the outlying radio stations. Most of the bucket seats were occupied by approximately a dozen or so scared-looking enlisted men, whose faces reflected their doubts regarding the imminent takeoff. Captain Lewis and Goerig moved into two adjoining seats and buckled themselves in. A husky, red haired co-pilot came back to check over the situation.

Upon returning to the cockpit, he briskly turned his head around with an unreassuring smile and remarked, "Well, wish us luck." It was definitely not a sign of encouragement. George crossed himself and said a short prayer.

As the howling engines were revved up, the whole plane shook and seemed to groan. Presently the transport moved into position and started to roll forward. As it gained momentum down the runway, Goerig noticed the gradual slope of a hill directly ahead. The ground began going by rapidly while the tortured motors wailed. As they neared the end of the airstrip, the moment of greatest danger, the pilot finally managed to lift the overladen plane off the asphalt and barely skim over the tops of some scrubby bushes. A few moments later, the door to the cockpit opened and the co-pilot came back out. He forced a sickly grin and shakily announced, "We were damn lucky."

Holding up two fingers in a victory sign, he returned to his seat. Goerig fleetingly glanced around at his fellow passengers and noted a few of them crossing themselves in grateful thanks, while others anxiously looked down at the receding landscape.

After an hour's flying time, the transport approached the small town of Liangshan. The setting sun seemed to wink at the relieved passengers as it slid behind the horizon. They had finally made it safely. The tired plane, with flaps down, settled on the runway and eventually came to a screeching halt, as the smoking wheels obediently reacted to its stubborn brakes.

After they had disembarked, Captain Lewis joined the others in search of some food and a place to bunk down for the night. It had been a strenuous trip.

It was November 17th, 1944. Liangshan was the first stop on the trip to Goerig's eventual destination, Laifeng. Captain Lewis had started the expansion of the existing runway and wanted to orient the three recruits to the construction methods of the Chinese contractors. George was looking forward to the new challenge he would shortly be faced with. He figured that with such an adept teacher, he would prove himself a willing and eager pupil.

The two enlisted men who had accompanied him on the trip from Chungking were being processed by an officer who was making arrangements for them on their new assignments. In the meantime, the captain and the private were met outside the engineering office by a tall, lanky sergeant with a ruddy, beaming face. He was the captain's assistant on the base.

"Just call me John," he announced. "Smith is the last name, but we never use it around here." They all shook hands. "How are you doing, Captain?"

"Don't worry about how the hell I'm doing. How is the job going? Are you still shackin' up with that slant-eyed mistress of yours?"

George looked surprised at the sudden familiarity between the two men.

"Oh, come on now, Captain, you know that I have been saving her for you," replied the sergeant with a feigned look of disbelief.

"I know what you'd save for me, probably her mother," Lewis snapped.

Smith quipped back, "To each his own, sir."

As they threw their bags in the back of the waiting jeep, John gunned the motor while Goerig had a hunch he was in for a fast trip. He wasn't disappointed. In practically no time, they had crossed the airstrip and were coming to a squealing halt in front of the base headquarters.

"All out!" yelled the sergeant. "Come on, George, I'll show you our humble quarters while our supreme commander takes over his luxurious suite in the officers' mansion."

John ducked his head as the captain gave him a playful swing. "Dammit, John. Have some respect for your elders."

"I do sir, I do!" he wailed as he straightened up.

Laughingly, he grabbed Lewis's duffel bag as Goerig had a pleasant feeling he was going to enjoy the sergeant's company during his brief stay in Liangshan.

Later as the noncom and George checked into the headquarters' office, the latter was introduced to a short, good-looking Chinese, who seemed to be about thirty-five years old. He was the hotel manager, and his name was Soo Yung.

"Now, Soo, you take really good care of Mister Goerig while he is here. He might be only a private, but as far as we are concerned, he is a great big man in our organization."

Sergeant stressed his point by wagging his index finger under the manager's nose.

"Will do, will do, Sergeant Smith." Turning to Goerig, he smiled. "Please come with me, Mister Goerig, and I will show you around the camp area."

The man's natural command of the English language startled George. He learned later that the Chinese national had graduated from an American university in Shanghai. The two were soon to become close friends during his month's stay in Liangshan.

One night after supper, Soo approached the private as he walked out of the mess hall. "Would you like to join me in an evening's stroll?" he hesitantly asked.

"Love to," was the answer, "you lead the way. I'm a foreigner here, you know."

The manager laughed and with a quick, backward glance, whispered, "We are going to be followed, but you don't have to worry about it."

George hesitated and looked back. "What do you mean, we'll be followed?"

As the two continued on the way towards town, Goerig soon learned the facts about a false democracy that was supposed to represent to the world a free and popular government. That country was Nationalist China. Actually, the controlling faction was limited to probably less than 1 percent of the hundreds of millions struggling Chinese who were trying to eke out a passable living from the overworked soil of the land.

While Soo continued in a low voice, George glanced back again and then noticed two men maintaining a discreet distance behind them.

"They have spies everywhere. When I go back to the hostel, I will probably be interrogated about our meeting and what we discussed. However, I feel I have to talk with somebody. Mister Goerig, our government is bad, really bad. The people who control everything in the Kuomintang regime are very corrupt and they bleed my people of all they can get. Our Generalissimo, Chiang Kai-shek, was supposed to be the savior of the country after all the provincial wars we have gone through. You cannot imagine what is really going on here. He is surrounded by a small group of influential men who want to dominate my people and take everything they can from them."

Goerig was appalled at the sudden frankness of what he was hearing from the man.

With a frightened expression on his face, Soo again looked back over his shoulder. "Someday there will be a change after the war is over. The communists will defeat the Kuomintang. Wait and see."

George still couldn't believe his ears.

The manager continued. "Mao Tse-sung, the leader of the outlawed party, is now preparing to eventually chase out the present government of China. It will not be long after the war is over."

The sudden impact of what he had heard left the private in a complete daze. He had had no knowledge of the vicious inner struggle being waged in the confines of China.

Soo calmly went on. "Complete convoys of your trucks, driven by specially assigned Chinese soldiers, have completely disappeared within a short distance of a few miles. The trucks are dismantled and the parts are hidden so that when the real war for the control of this land begins, the Generalissimo will be able to reassemble the shipment and use it in his fight against the communists." He hesitated. "I think I have spoken enough now. Perhaps we had better go back. Please never mention anything we have discussed tonight."

Goerig solemnly promised his newfound friend, "It will be strictly between the two of us."

As they turned to go back, the two dim figures who had been following them disappeared behind the trees lining the sides of the road. George had received his first indoctrination into the vast web of intrigue and the corrupt background behind the so-called peoples' government. He was to learn much more later. One general by the name of Stilwell had the guts enough to try and convince the bureaucrats back in Washington, DC, that the Americans were being taken by one General Massimo "Peanut Head"! His attempts to awaken the government to face the facts fell on deaf ears. So, what else was new? It wasn't long in coming.

Goerig had been wondering what had ever happened with Helen's pregnancy. Her letters came through fairly regularly. She informed her husband that a certain portion of her anatomy had been changing in size and she no longer had the slender figure he had become accustomed to.

"Your wife just had an eight-pound boy," John Smith said after he had rushed over from the headquarters' office as soon as he'd received the report from the Red Cross over the base radio. The expected news left Goerig limp. John reached past George and pulled out a bottle of bourbon from under the mattress on his bed.

"This one is on me. You beat me to it, George. Congratulations."

The proud new father picked up his cup of the hastily poured liquor and happily announced, "His name will be Acey, for Albert Charles Goerig, just like his grandfather."

It was the thirtieth day of November, nineteen hundred and forty-four. Four cups were raised in unison, two days after his boy had been born. They also drank to the Red Cross, which had only been late by two days. Following the first toast, the evening went by rapidly until George began feeling no pain. His newfound friends helped him into bed, and he went blissfully to sleep.

"Come on, come on, let's get our asses on the way. They're not going to hold that plane forever!" shouted Captain Lewis, as Goerig was trying to cram the last piece of clothing into his barracks bag.

"Okay, okay, take it easy, sir. I'll be right with you. You know you can't go without me."

"The hell I can't!" he barked. "You're no big shot yet. Wait until you've done something worthwhile."

George slung the huge bag over his shoulder and trudged toward the ever-waiting jeep. Enshih was coming next.

═

The memory of that small town was vague. However, Goerig did remember meeting one outstanding personality by the name of Father Borge. He was a Roman Catholic priest from Belgium. His stay in China had lasted over thirty years, and he was preparing to return to his homeland as soon as the war was over. He was a tall, huskily built man with silver gray hair dominating a florid face and a radiant smile. Goerig liked him instantly. He spoke five languages fluently and his English was flawless.

"George, how do you like China?" the priest asked.

"Fine, Father, at least what I have seen of it."

He gave a hearty laugh and continued. "Yes, there is a lot of country in China, and during my time here, I have been over most of it. It has been a rough job trying to convert so many heathens, but it does have satisfying results after a while. I am anxious to get home, however, and see what kind of shape my country is in now. We are grateful to your marvelous troops for helping drive out those damn krauts." The priest momentarily paused and looked skyward. "Pardon me, Lord, but I do get mad now and then. Please forgive me."

The father then put his arm around George's shoulder and announced, "Tonight, you will be my guest for dinner. I also think I might have some special wine to help chase away the evil spirits."

Captain Lewis had been invited out by the commanding officer of the base and Goerig's evening was free. It turned out to be the highlight of his short tour through the center of China. After dinner, the Father and the private sat down comfortably in two overstuffed leather chairs before a roaring fire in the host's simple living room. A Chinese houseboy stood in the background ready to replenish the wine glasses the two were sipping from.

Father Borge began, "I will be leaving here soon. I guess I am too outspoken. The Generalissimo has ordered me out of the country because he thinks I talk too much, I guess." He twirled the empty wine glass in his hand. "I love this country and its people. I will be happy to go home, but my work is not finished here. Whether you know it or not, George, the communists under Mao Tse-Sung will move in after the war with the Japanese is over. It is inevitable. At the present time, we have a very corrupt government that has been bleeding their people mercilessly."

The private silently recalled the same thoughts of his friend, Soo, in Liangshan.

"But Father, these people need you," he pleaded.

The priest smiled. "There will be others to take my place." Then he paused thoughtfully. Standing up, he reached over for George's glass.

"One more short drink and we will call it a night. I have enjoyed your company."

"I certainly have enjoyed yours, Father," the private answered, "and I hope you have a pleasant trip home."

As he walked out into the brisk air of the evening, Goerig could only reflect. What a wonderful person. It's too bad the world doesn't have more of them.

When he returned to his temporary barracks, there was a note on his bunk. "We leave at eight o'clock in the morning for Laifeng. Be there." It was signed, "Your boss."

George laughed, undressed, and sleepily climbed in between the fresh, inviting sheets. Momentarily, before closing his eyes, the private warmly recalled the beautiful words he would never forget: RSVP CHINA. At last, they had finally come true.

CHAPTER SIX

The portable alarm clock was ringing angrily and threatening to bounce off the nightstand as George sleepily groped for it. He sat up and shook his head. The after-effects of the previous evening's wine had dimmed his thinking. Where was he? Finally, it dawned on him. It still had to be Enshih, and he had better not keep the captain waiting. After hurriedly shaving and washing up, the private headed for the mess hall. After a quick breakfast of ham and eggs, he and the captain went in search of the motor pool, where they were to obtain their last means of transportation in the form of a durable jeep. Since gas was a scarce commodity on the road to Laifeng, Lewis was going to make certain he had an ample supply. For that purpose, he acquired four additional cans of the precious fluid.

Shortly after all the preparations had been made, the two men happily left their overnight stop. Despite repeated warnings of the possibility of meeting Chinese bandits along the way, they thought the possibility of that actually happening was a remote one, and they gave it little thought. The reassuring fact that they wore sidearms and carried carbines gave them a false sense of security at the same time that it appealed to their adventurous nature.

Eventually the road to their destination became dangerously narrow and winding. After passing through the outskirts of a small town that, surprisingly, appeared deserted, the two men came upon a group of shabbily dressed, local peasants accompanied by four soldiers in military garb. A bearded man knelt on the ground before them, his hands tightly bound behind his back. As the jeep approached, Goerig applied the brakes and both men curiously climbed out. It appeared they were about to witness an example of Chinese justice.

One of the soldiers was pointing a pistol at the head of the kneeling prisoner. Suddenly, he fired two shots at close range. With blood streaming from each side of his head, the unfortunate victim fell forward and began a frantic writhing on the ground.

Captain Lewis, his face showing utter contempt, and outraged by such a display of inhuman cruelty, boldly moved forward and motioned for the uniformed man to move aside. Calmly removing the forty-five from his holster, he proceeded to mercifully end the agonized man's sufferings. The two then hurriedly returned to the jeep, silently hoping they had not jeopardized the protocol of the United States government. Their departure left a stunned and bewildered group of Chinese with gaping mouths, staring at the cloud of dust raised by the quickly departing jeep.

After an hour of cautious driving, the two men suddenly came upon a group of four slovenly clad, disorderly peasants carrying rifles. Lewis immediately discerned that here were some of the so-called bandits he had been forewarned about.

Without a pause, he yelled, "Step on it!" Needing no further encouragement, George pushed down hard on the gas pedal and slammed his palm on the horn. The rugged little vehicle responded immediately and lurched threateningly toward the bandits.

Caught by surprise, the bewildered men were thrown into a temporary state of confusion as some of them quickly leaped into the adjacent ditches, leaving a narrow, broken path among the remainder. The suddenness of the approach and their natural instinct for survival in the face of the barreling vehicle gave the bandits little chance to take advantage of the situation. However, as the jeep sped down the dirt road, several shots rang out. One bullet managed to hit its target and subsequently shattered the windshield of the careening Willys.

It had slightly grazed the captain's steel helmet as the older man clung desperately to the bottom of the canvas-covered seat.

"Goddamn it. I said move this rig, fast!"

"What the hell do you think I'm doing?" hollered the shaking and frightened enlisted man, his knuckles turning white as he frantically gripped the loose steering wheel.

The serenity of the picturesque countryside had been rudely disrupted by the brief, unexpected encounter. After a few agonizing moments, the cowering captain slowly raised his head and hesitantly glanced back at the billowing cloud of dust rising behind them. Finally straightening up, he muttered, "Okay, okay, I think we can take it easy now, a little. We're out of range and they're on foot. Thank God! Now I know why that major back in Enshih was serious when he warned us about the possibility of running into some stray Chinese bandits. I thought he was kidding. Those crazy bastards back there have no respect for the American army."

The trembling private, still visibly shaken but managing to gain control of himself, turned his head and shouted over the accelerated roar of the engine, "Perhaps, they didn't see your captain bars, sir!"

Lewis's round, florid face, ridiculously framed by the oversized helmet, broke into a feeble grin as he began to explain to his aide, in a serious tone, "George, consider yourself lucky. Those guys back there don't care about a damn thing. There are thousands of those thieving bands all over China. They live off the peasants. It is the only life they know. When the soldiers catch up with them, they are shot on the spot. So what? There are always many more to take their place."

The enlisted man automatically nodded his head in assent. Then, suddenly noticing a small creek that began paralleling the road ahead, he pointed toward it and looked pleadingly at his superior.

"How about if I pull off to the side of the road up there? I've got some important business to attend to."

"Be my guest," was the answer.

As the dusty jeep came to a screeching halt, Goerig leaned back and opened his barracks bags to draw out a towel. Then, digging a little deeper, he grasped a bar of soap. With those articles in hand, he climbed out of the jeep and started down the slight incline to the welcoming stream.

After a few moments, the captain stepped out into the road, leisurely stretching his legs. Walking over to the edge of the bank, he glanced down at the energetic, embarrassed private who was busily scrubbing his shorts in the slow-moving waters.

Silently chuckling to himself, the officer finally called down to his aide, "Well, I've heard the expression about somebody getting the hell scared out of them, but this is a new angle."

Then, noting the still-harried look on George's flushed face, the captain apologetically added, "Sorry, boy. I guess you really got scared. Don't let it bother you, though. So was I, but not quite so much, I guess."

Presently, a beaming sun broke out from behind a solitary cloud in the azure blue sky. Its welcoming warm rays seemed to ease the tension in Goerig's lean, tanned body as he paused momentarily and looked up at his superior.

"How about pulling out that bottle of booze I saw you stash away last night? I think we have something to be thankful for and right now should be a helluva good time for a little celebration. After all, we've only got about fifty miles to go, and we should be in good spirits when we get there. Can't let our future hosts think that a few bandits would ever worry us. How about it, sir?"

The answer came quickly. "You're damn right, boy. I think we deserve it. In fact, I know we do."

Going back to the jeep, the captain reached into his duffel bag and eagerly brought out a quart of scotch whiskey. Tenderly, he kissed it and proceeded to cautiously slide down the bank to where Goerig was naked and sitting unceremoniously with the towel draped over his shoulders. His shorts lay conveniently drying over a nearby boulder.

The private looked up and said with mock gratitude, "Captain, you are the greatest. I'm glad I came along." Then, he added more seriously, "You know, sir, this makes up for a helluva lot since I got drafted in this man's army."

After taking a swallow from the uncorked bottle, Lewis handed it to George. "You might as well sit back and enjoy this. It will probably be quite a while till you have any more booze as good as what we have here. In fact, I might just have a little snooze before we get going on our way."

Completely relaxed, the private began to silently reminisce about the adventurous past months during which he had been taken from a beautiful civilian life and thrown into the rigors of Army life. Then, briefly looking up to the sky, George fervently thanked his God for sparing him the trials and tribulations of a threatened general court martial. Yes, he had been very lucky. Those magic, golden words, "RSVP, China," had miraculously changed his unfortunate past into a glorious expected future.

CHAPTER SEVEN

Laifeng, their final destination, was similar to the other small towns they had encountered in China. Surrounded by a ten-foot wall, the main thoroughfare consisted of a curbed street, paved with bricks, that extended down the length of the bordering clapboard-faced buildings. It was very quiet, and the main area seemed practically deserted. Later, George was to learn that most activity took place on Market Day, once every week. It was then that the surrounding countryside would erupt with its many farmers and peasants. They would descend upon the town and sell their produce to the townspeople. The latter, in turn, would try and out-haggle their neighbors with varied stocks of crude merchandise. It was the big day.

The future home for the weary travelers was a short walk from Laifeng. It consisted of an impressive, two-hundred-year-old military compound that at one time or the other had comprised the headquarters of the various and ambitious small-time rulers of the local district.

Adjacent to the ancient compound and located over the floor of a natural valley was a three-thousand-foot airstrip. It had been constructed several years previously to accommodate the needs of the Flying Tigers. The runway was in sharp contrast to its centuries-old surroundings. This was to be the base of Private Goerig's future operations and his new home.

As the captain and George approached the arched entrance to the old structure, they were met at the gate by a genial-looking, middle-aged

George and Lieutenant Lee.

Chinese man dressed in a military uniform. He wore captain insignia and was accompanied by another officer whom they quickly learned was the official interpreter. He introduced himself as Lieutenant Lee, and his superior's name was Captain Ho Ka Jan.

After the formalities were over, the guests were taken on a brief tour of the compound, where George became acquainted with his future quarters. He was introduced to two young and grinning lads who had been chosen as his personal houseboys. Their names were Chen and Chang. It had been quite an honor for them as they had been specially selected from the ranks of the small garrison at the base.

A balding, elderly man was next presented as Goerig's personal cook. The latter proudly proceeded to show off his primitive but efficient kitchen facilities, which consisted primarily of two clay ovens. The top of each was concave and held two cast iron cooking pans, better known as wats.

It was on these that all meals were cooked with efficiency and skill. Hastily glancing back again at his new home, George thought to himself, "Man, how lucky can you get?"

Following a tasty and satisfying meal of soup, boiled chicken, mixed vegetables, and the inevitable steamed rice, the two Americans reluctantly left the table to attend to the task of moving Goerig's belongings into his new quarters. It didn't take very long, and afterward Captain Lewis decided it was time to turn in. The beds that were prepared for them seemed heavenly after the arduous jeep ride. It was not long before George was dreaming of his own new Shanghai-La, now a reality, due to his unforgettable RSVP message.

Goerig awoke to a beautiful morning with the sun already streaming in through the semi-shuttered windows. His captain, who was already up, hollered impatiently, "Get the hell out of bed, it's time for reveille!"

The private lazily rolled over and jokingly muttered, "Go to hell, I'm on vacation."

"Vacation be damned, you are just starting to do something for your private's pay. Before you finish here, I'll see to it that you have earned it too, boy."

Not knowing whether his boss was joking or not, George hurriedly threw back the cotton blankets and started to dress. A timid knock on the door was shortly followed by Chen and Chang entering, carrying two basins of hot water and towels draped over their arms. They placed the articles down on a stand and hesitated momentarily to see if there was anything else their new master might want. The captain thankfully waved them out as George started digging in his barracks bag for his toilet case. Finally, dumping everything on the floor, he managed to find it.

"Best room service in China." Goerig laughed. "I wonder how the rest of the privates are making out. If my old CO could only see me now."

Methodically lathering his face, Captain Lewis hesitated and then turned to his new aide. "You really hate that guy, don't you?"

George, grinningly looked up. "I don't hate anybody this morning. I'm too damn happy, and by the time I'm finished building up this place, we're going to have the best air base in China. Chennault and his Flying Tigers are going to love us."

"Correction, boy," Lewis retorted, "you are now in the Fourteenth Air Force. The Flying Tigers are a thing of the past. You might as well know that right now. This is not going to be a fighter base, but a home for reconnaissance 'eye spies.' You might not realize it," he continued in a serious tone," but the Japs have big ideas about taking over this section of China. We are here to keep a check on the activities of their ground forces and what air bases they might want to take over in the meantime. It may not sound too romantic to you in that it involves no part in the real action, but you still have a damn responsible job on your hands. After constructing the new campsite, get ready to make room for about thirty thousand Chinese laborers out there extending that runway and widening it."

The captain resumed shaving.

"Thirty thousand coolies out there?" the private asked incredulously. "Where the hell are they all going to sleep and eat?"

Portion of 30,000 Chinese coolees working on the runway.

His superior laughed. "Clever people, these Chinese. They'll surprise you, George, you are in for quite an education in the Oriental ways of construction. You might as well forget all about your dozers, steam shovels, graders, rock crushers, and the American way of getting things done. I'm not sure, myself, how the hell they manage, but I do know that it is up to us to see that they get the job done right and in the shortest time possible. The Japs aren't going to sit back and wait. They are pushing ahead fast, and Chiang's motley crew of soldiers won't be too much opposition if the past is any indication of their capabilities. Our boys are plenty busy enough in the Pacific and in Europe to worry about this damn patch of rice paddies. We are here to find out what they plan on doing in this sector and how fast they are going to do it."

Goerig meekly replied, "Yes sir, I understand. I assure you that I'll do my best."

The captain was busily brushing his close-cropped hair while trying to get some image from the cracked, faded mirror hanging on the wall. Finally, he turned and looked at George's receding hairline and the growing spot of baldness crowning his head.

"George, you are going to be a novelty out here. Perhaps, you can make a deal with some of the Chinese gals with their long hair and have one of them make up a toupee for you. You know there was quite a business going on in China before the war. Women's hair was exported by the ton to satisfy the needs of balding men in the United States.

Goerig disdainfully replied, "Hell, I've been losing my hair since I was in college. The gals still love me, though. I'm getting used to being bald. It gives me a distinguished look. Perhaps the Chinese will think I'm a lot older than twenty-six. Maybe I'll get more respect."

Lewis laughed again while applying an aromatic lotion to his face. Then, finally putting the bottle down, he impatiently hollered, "Come on, boy, finish up or we'll be late for breakfast!"

The captain opened the door and George followed him into the spacious courtyard. Suddenly, a large, black rooster with a red, quivering comb emerged from under the building, frantically chasing a frightened little bantam hen.

Momentarily startled, Goerig quipped, "Watch China grow." He then recalled the crowing sounds that had woken him up about daybreak. An attitude of defiance seemed natural to all living creatures.

While crossing the hard, clay-packed courtyard, George noticed several soldiers tending the shrubbery-bound area. A few looked up as they passed and, raising their hands with thumb extended upward, chorused a familiar expression, "Ding hao, ding hao!" It meant, "Very good, very good."

Having heard the words before and realizing the men were merely trying to convey their simple feelings towards the American guests, they waved back. Later, the opposite of the phrase was explained to George. It was "boo hao," meaning very bad. His initiation into the Chinese language was off to a booming start.

As they sat down at the table, which was to become a daily ritual, the two guests were pleasantly surprised at the table setting. Before them were knives, forks, and spoons laid out with cups filled with steaming coffee. A ceramic vase filled with freshly picked flowers had been placed in the middle of the table.

"Over sunny?" cackled the wizened chef as he cracked several eggs over the heated wat.

The captain winked in amazement. "How about that? Strictly stateside. Over easy," he answered.

"Okay," came the response.

Shortly, plates with beaming eggs, strips of crisp bacon, and buttered toast were placed before them. The old cook stood patiently aside as the captain and the private began eating.

"Okay?" he hesitantly asked.

"Wonderful," was the answer. "Couldn't be better."

Unobtrusively, a smiling Lieutenant Lee sidled up to the table. "Good morning. Is everything satisfactory?" he asked.

Captain Lewis acknowledged his greeting and then politely inquired, "Great, but where on earth did you find that terrific cook? He didn't learn American ways of cooking like this around here."

Lee laughed and then replied, "Foo Sung came from Shanghai, four or maybe five years ago. He did not like working for the Japanese. He had been a chef for a large hotel back there. We were fortunate to find him. As you noticed, he speaks a little English."

Coffee cups were refilled, and the Chinese lieutenant joined in the discussion of the program for the day. Captain Lewis initiated the talk.

"Okay, the transport plane will be coming in around four o'clock this afternoon. I'll leave at that time, and then, George, you'll be on your own. First of all, we'll have to pick out the spot for the campsite. Lieutenant, we could use a couple of your men to help in staking out the area. I have a hundred-foot tape and some chalk line. With these we can lay out the definite locations for the squadron office, mess hall, and the tent floors."

The captain hesitated as though he was trying to recall an item that had slipped his mind.

"Oh, yes, the latrine. We can't forget that. I know it is essential for your 'honey bucket' boys. They have to have their fertilizer." He suddenly shuddered at the thought of eating food that had been treated with human excrement.

He turned toward Lee. "Not many of the big contactors in Chungking are too interested in the building portion of the work coming up, so we'll have to contact some local men for that portion of the contract."

Lee nodded his head as Lewis continued, "I'll get the general layout plans and we'll be on our way."

The captain excused himself and went back over to the room where he had spent the night. He shortly returned with a roll of the plans under his arm. George walked over to his jeep and started the engine. After some coughing and sputtering, the motor warmed up to a steady rhythm. Lewis jumped in, followed by the Chinese lieutenant. The trio passed through the arched entrance of the compound and wound down a rutted, dirt road. As they approached the runway, Lee pointed toward a picturesque vale lying between two small hills, approximately a thousand feet from the center of the air strip.

Slipping the gears into four-wheel drive, Goerig pressed down on the accelerator and headed for the sharp incline towards the indicated campsite.

"Hang on!" he shouted over the screaming roar of the engine as the jeep bounced and lurched forward up the grass-covered hill. Then with a final burst of its mechanical energy, the trio found themselves looking over a mound landscape marked by many mounds.

"What the hell are those?" hollered the captain.

"Graves," replied the lieutenant. "Many years old, covered with stones to protect the dead Chinese from the evil spirits. An old Chinese custom."

"How deep are they buried?" asked Lewis.

"Five, maybe six feet. No worry. Nobody will bother. China is at war. The spirits will go away. We can fix the camp here. There is plenty of space outside the graves.

The captain then became aware of a portion of the area that had no mounds. It seemed large enough for the entire campsite. Lewis quickly spread out the roll of plans.

"Alright," he muttered, "let's get to work." Pointing to the foremost section of the vale, Lewis continued, "We'll spot the office there and the mess hall will be about fifty feet to the north of it. Starting about thirty feet parallel to the office and the mess hall, let's align the tent sites in orderly rows with about ten feet between them."

Noting a small, dried-up creek bed winding its course through the center of the area, he took one cautionary look at the gathering clouds. "Got to plan on some culverts under the pathways. Eight-inch tile should take care of any cloud burst. We'll spot the 'crapper' over on that far corner and that should take care of this site."

He turned towards his aide. "Well, George, do you think you can handle this big engineering deal after I'm gone?"

The private quickly assured his superior. "Don't you worry about a thing, Captain. Consider it practically done."

Glancing over at Lieutenant Lee, Goerig added, "With such fine help around here at my disposal, we can tackle anything. How about it, sir?"

Lee grinned and nodded approvingly.

Lewis then pointed to the top of the closest hill. "Okay, now let's get our fannies up there and lay out a location for the radio station. By the way, how do we get up there without climbing our butts off?"

"There is a small road around the other side," said Lee. "It will be easy with the jeep. I will show you."

The road he pointed out was more like a mountain goat's trail. However, with its four wheels clawing at the steep terrain, the tough little Willys eventually topped the crest of the hill. A leveled area provided ample turning-around space, and Captain Lewis beamed.

"Perfect." His eyes approvingly roamed over the unobstructed landscape. "Couldn't ask for a better set-up. Shouldn't have any atmospheric interference up here. Okay, let's get back!" he impatiently barked.

The three began the perilous descent down the treacherous slope. Finally, after much sliding and steady braking, the jeep managed to roll down to the floor of the valley. From that point, the group started a circuitous route of the grass-covered runway. Occasionally, the captain would stop the jeep and climb out. With a pick in his hands, he would start digging into the hard-packed rocky ground in order to determine its actual depth. After approximately twenty such testings, during which he was relieved by the other two at a certain point, they headed back to the compound.

Upon arriving outside the courtyard, George swung the jeep over to the parking spot. They all climbed out and started for Lieutenant Lee's office. The plans were spread out on a makeshift drafting table as Lewis began to draw out the campsite locations. A soldier appeared in the doorway and beckoned to Lieutenant Lee. The latter nodded his head and excused himself from the room.

Taking a ruler in his hand and checking the contour lines marked out on the plans, the captain proceeded to lay out the locations of the various buildings and tent sites. Paths were drawn in and the necessary culverts indicated. Within an hour's time, a rough sketch emerged of the overall project. Goerig silently marveled at his boss's dexterity and quietly envied his engineering capabilities.

Finally looking up from his crouched position over the table, Lewis began, "As you can see, I have approximated the location of the buildings in regard to the contour lines. This is to alleviate any unnecessary excavation, which would only add to the cost and delay. This will suffice for the time being."

Then, spreading out a smaller set of plans consisting of various building designs, he continued, "These are duplicate sets of plans we have in the main office at Chungking. Our next job is to call for bids on the buildings. The contractors will be governed by these plans and accompanying specifications. Once the actual work is started here in Laifeng on this portion of the overall project, you will have all the information needed to cover the inspection on all phases of the work. Comprehende, Private Goerig?"

"Si, si, sir," George mockingly answered. "Not to change the subject, but don't you think that being placed in charge of an undertaking as important as this should warrant a rank like sergeant or something?" He winked, hoping it might have an appealing affect.

The effect was instantaneous.

"Private Goerig, you once were a sergeant and look at all the trouble it got you into. Why don't you just bide your time and, perhaps if you do a good job and stay out of trouble, I will try and get a stripe for you."

"Oh gee, sir, that would be great," Goerig sardonically replied. "But do you actually think that would be sufficient to create enough face for me to get the respect of the Chinese?"

With a wry smile, the captain answered, "American money is what makes 'face' around here, and as long as we are the official representatives responsible for Uncle Sam's dough, we'll have a lot of face and respect. I know of your past civilian qualifications and your experience in the construction field, and I believe you are capable of marshalling your talents to help meet our responsibilities with the Chinese."

He paused a moment and then continued, "Captain Ho Ka Jan and Lieutenant Lee appear to be very sincere men. I don't believe the corruption, which is beginning to be shown by the Kuomintang Party, has quite begun to have any effect on these officers. They seem to be very frank and honest in their actions. In any case, if you have any difficulties with the contractors, I'm sure you can count on their support. Remember, Captain Ho is the boss man around this base."

Goerig hesitated to further press his case for a higher rank for the time being.

Suddenly, Lewis's expression changed from officious to sincere.

"George, believe me, if you don't let me down here, I'll do everything within my power to see that you regain your rank and maybe something a little extra."

The private nodded and reluctantly decided to drop the matter. If he knew what the captain was going to do for him about eight months later, George would have been a very happy person.

"I'm hungry," growled the officer as he quickly changed the subject. "Let's go over and case the kitchen. Maybe our chef has something he can dish up in a hurry."

He led the way out of the office into the courtyard. Then looking at his watch, Lewis scanned the cumulous clouds gathering overhead. Wistfully, he mentioned, "Hope that plane can make it here by four o'clock. I have no great desire to fly around this country in the dark."

As if in answer to his personal wish, a faint droning sound came to their attention. The two ran out of the courtyard and over to the edge of the bank, straining their eyes skyward. Within a few moments, the familiar sight of the wings and the fuselage of a C-47 broke through the grayish overcast sky and began circling the diminutive field. Gradually, as it lost altitude, the transport glided in from a sharp descent to a perfect landing.

By this time, Captain Lewis had rushed back to George's room for his meager belongings. Pausing to grab his lightened briefcase, he headed for the jeep. Goerig had already started the sputtering engine, and as the officer jumped into the back, they started down the narrow dirt lane toward the waiting plane.

"Be sure and tell Captain Ho and Lieutenant Lee I'm sorry I didn't have the time to thank them for the hospitality!" he hollered over the roar of the motor. "You be sure and do that, and I'll keep you posted on the contract bid results. Should get them in a week or so. In the meantime, have Lee stake out the exact location of the buildings and the tent sites that I laid out in the plans. If you have any serious problems arise, you can always contact me through the radio transmitter."

After Lewis tried but failed to recall a few more bits of fatherly advice, which Goerig deemed unnecessary, they pulled up alongside of the waiting aircraft with its two motors noisily idling.

A bushy haired, frowning lad dressed in a jump suit heavily stained with grease and motor oil was nervously standing by the door ramp.

"If you don't mind, sir," he apologized unnecessarily, "we're in a sort of a hurry. Gets dark pretty early this time of the year. Our pilot wants to get back to Chungking as soon as possible."

"Be right with you," answered the captain as he leaped over the side of the vehicle and started for the open door. With a quick turn of his head, he shouted, "It's all yours, George, take good care of it!"

With a final wave of his hand, Lewis boarded, the seemingly impatient "workhorse of the war," the C-47. The crew chief followed with alacrity, pulling the ramp up behind him.

The tortured twin engines screamed as the advanced throttle forced new energy into their hot innards. Slowly, like a bird with outstretched wings, the plane lurched forward. Billowing, swirling clouds of dust rose up to form a great mass, as though the propellers were even showing their contempt for Goerig's glorious field. The rising plane then gracefully cleared the small grassy knoll at the far end of the runway and quickly disappeared into the waiting folds of the overcast clouds. Private Goerig was on his own. He had officially, finally answered the RSVP request of General Clare Chennault. Now the rest was up to him.

CHAPTER EIGHT

It was shortly after George's arrival in Laifeng when he approached Lieutenant Lee and said, "Sir, I am a Christian. To be more explicit, I am of the Roman Catholic faith. Would it be possible that there is a Catholic missionary living here in Laifeng?"

It was obvious that the officer was not a Catholic as he pondered for a moment before finally answering, "Yes, there is a priest here. He lives on the far side of town. I would be happy to send one of your boys to take you there."

George warmly thanked him. "I have some free time now. Could Chen show me the way?"

"Certainly." He called over to the houseboy who had been attentively standing to one side. A brief discussion followed. Chen nodded his head, inadvertently drawing attention to his bowl-shaped haircut, and went back to his master's room. When he emerged, he handed Goerig his flight Jacket and they started walking through the portal of the compound.

The trip down the main thoroughfare of Laifeng was very interesting. Since it was not market day, the street was practically empty with the exception of a few persons dressed in the Mandarin style, who courteously bowed as the two passed by.

Chen, in his temporary new role as a guide for his illustrious master, was enjoying the position tremendously.

The wooden clap-board faced buildings they passed were intriguing, and George silently wondered what type of activity could be going on behind their weathered facades. Before long, they reached the walled outskirts of the small town. As the two walked down an elevated dirt path with the flooded rice paddies on each side, Chen pointed to a medium-size house on the crest of an adjoining hill. They turned off on a narrower lane leading up to their destination. Shortly, the man and the boy were met by a short, black frocked, smiling father, who had come down to meet them. He greeted George. "Hello, welcome."

Goerig was momentarily startled by the fact that the priest spoke English. Then he suddenly realized that during the years of study that had qualified him for the robes he wore, his education had probably covered many languages.

His name was Father Loo. He motioned for the two to come into his home. Chen dutifully bowed his head and turned to go. Goerig suddenly felt lost.

"Wait a minute, boy. We go back together. Go sit down on that bench over there. I won't be long."

The priest quickly interpreted the words, and the lad obediently walked over and happily sat down. Upon entering the humble abode, George was met by two smiling women dressed in their Chinese garb.

"Mister George"—a name he would come to be known by during his stay at Laifeng—"please meet my mother and my sister."

Goerig suddenly felt relieved upon learning that his future confessor was not a married man. He looked around the simple room. A small unpretentious altar was set at one side, and the Chinese furniture was conveniently located in its proper place.

As they sat down in the straight-backed chairs, a pot of tea and cups were placed on a small round table before them. A short period of expected silence was broken by Father Loo.

"Welcome to Laifeng," he began. "I have been studying on my English since I heard about your arrival. I did not know you were a Catholic. but I hoped so. This is really a pleasant surprise."

"Father, it is as much as a surprise to me that I have found a Catholic priest who speaks English in such an out-of-the-way place. It makes me very happy and relieved that I may be able to attend mass and possibly take Holy Communion every week."

George was not prepared when his host asked him, "Can you serve mass?"

"Dominum vobiscum, et cum spiritu tuo," the private proudly answered.

Father laughed after explaining a few words in interpretation to his attentive family members.

Goerig continued, "Father, I believe I am a little rusty or should I say out of practice on the serving part of my religion. My Latin is not as good as it ought to be."

"Mister George, there is no problem. I have been answering myself for many years. I would welcome your company at the Holy Mass."

"I'll take a stab at it, Father."

The next hour had passed rapidly in pleasant conversation when George looked down at his watch and said reluctantly, "I didn't realize it was so late. I must be getting back for supper. It certainly has been a pleasure."

Rising from his chair, he nodded to the eager, smiling faces of the priest's mother and sister. "Please thank them for their marvelous hospitality. I hope to see you all again next Sunday."

Father Loo followed George to the door. Grasping his hand, he warmly murmured, "God bless you."

"Thank you, Father."

As Goerig left the priest's home, he was joined by his houseboy and the two started down the hill. Suddenly the private stopped and looked at his servant's radiant face.

"Chen, you little heathen bastard, I should try and convert you."

The lad started to grin as he turned towards his master. Not understanding a word that had been spoken, he promptly raised his hand with an extended thumb pointing upward. "Ding hao, ding hao." Then he innocently asked, "Was a mean, 'bastard'?"

They continued on their way.

For three weeks, George attended Sunday Mass, and he felt very rewarded in the contentment that came with feeling closer to his God and the wonderful satisfaction of receiving Holy Communion. In the meantime, he had invited Father Loo to come over to the compound. One bright, sunny day, the priest arrived with a very solemn expression on his face. As they sat down in George's room, Chen brought in the customary pot of tea. After a few cordial words had been exchanged, the private waited for the Father to speak. He had been looking down at the floor, and it was apparent something had been bothering him. Finally, raising his head, he sadly announced, "Mister George, I have been told that I will not be able to visit with you again."

Goerig couldn't believe his ears. "What the hell? Pardon me, Father, but what do you mean? You can come here anytime you want to. Now, you just sit here while I go out and have a talk with a couple of my friends outside in their office. Don't worry." George started toward the door.

The priest hastily got to his feet. "Please, Mister George, you will only make things harder for me." Pleadingly, he looked at his host. "I do enjoy being with you. However, after you are gone from Laifeng, I still have to live here. Our mortal lives are governed by the Koumintang and we are at their mercy."

George thought back to his visit with Father Borge in Enshih and the priest's prophetic words about Chiang Kai-Shek. "He does not want any civilian Chinese to be friends with any member of the United States Armed Forces."

Slowly turning back, Goerig sat down next to a sad-faced but very relieved priest. "Okay, Father, you know best. I'll be at mass tomorrow."

The priest's expressions brightened, as he stood up. "I will see you then, son."

Father Loo walked out of the compound, and with his black robe fluttering in the light breeze, sadly waved goodbye.

CHAPTER NINE

It was not long before Private Goerig realized that Captain Ho Ka Jan would be a tremendous asset in some of his dealings with the varied and unknown factors involved in the problems the private would have to contend with. After the departure of Captain Lewis and the receipt of the bids for the first phase of the project, George had had time to become better acquainted with the station master, his aides, and his family. The station master's subordinates were comprised of Lieutenant Lee and another officer, whose main duty was the maintenance of the air base.

The family was something else. His wife was a petite lady with four lovely, disciplined children ranging in age from one to seven. The youngest lad needed no diapers, having the back of his sagging pants split up the middle for reasons of expediency.

Regarding the future construction work, the captain was an ardent participant in the discussions which Lee and the private had concerning the exigencies which might arise in their dealings with the Chinese contractors and their multitude of coolie laborers. Occasionally, Ho would politely interrupt the conversations and ask pertinent questions of the lieutenant, which Lee would then pass on to Goerig.

In turn, he would express his thoughts, and the three-way conference would usually wind up with everyone in accord.

Approximately two weeks had passed when a courier finally arrived from Chungking with the official results of the first competitive bids on the campsite, buildings, and furniture. They were as follows (amounts shown are in Chinese Nationalist dollars):

ITEMS	UNIT PRICES		
CONTRACTORS	KAO YI SUN	CHIANG TAI	YUN CHIN
SOUARDRON HEADQUARTERS	876,300	900,398	942,223
MESS HALL	1,089,21616	1,103,240	1,213,952
RADIO STATION	736,875	816,738	782,310
STOVE	272,280	281	273,650
TOTALS	2,974,699	2,820,376	2,212,135

ITEMS	UNIT PRICES		
CONTRACTORS	KAO YI SUN	CHIANG TAI	YUN CHIN
ITEM TENT	69,024	64,163	70,330
DOUBLE BEDS	11,890	12,000	12,100
CHAIRS	2,780	3,200	2,400
WARDROBES	7,300	7,400	7,380
TABLES	6,000	6,300	6,400

After evaluating the bids, Goerig was naturally at a loss to comprehend the prices quoted in relation to the actual value of the different items bid upon. Having no past criterion to fall back on, he felt thankful that the authority to award the contract was in somebody else's capable hands.

As it eventually turned out, the low bidder was from Chungking, as were the others. None of the contractors had been down to inspect the site prior to submitting their quotations. The private was, therefore, anxiously looking forward to meeting with the representatives of the successful construction firm.

Several days had passed when Mr. Kao Yi Sun himself finally arrived in Laifeng. He was a short, mild, and rather inconspicuous man with close-cropped hair. He had an engaging smile and surprisingly young looking to be a full-fledged contractor. In good English, he explained that he had been a college student at one time in Shanghai before the Japanese takeover. He was accompanied by two unpretentious-looking men dressed in Chinese garb, whom he presented as his supervisors.

When formalities were over, Goerig and Lee drove Mr. Kao to the proposed campsite, which by now had been accurately staked out. The contractor was asked when he could begin his operations.

"Mollow, okay?" he said, looking quizzically at George.

"Wonderful" was the response. "The sooner, the better."

Lumber yards were an unknown luxury in this sector of China. In fact, in practically all of China. Goerig was therefore looking forward to observing the Chinese technique used in acquiring the rough lumber needed for the various phases of their building construction. It wasn't long before he became indoctrinated into that portion of their modus operandi.

Trees cut from surrounding hills produced the logs that were then hauled to the campsite. The logs were next placed in improvised vises while two laborers proceeded to saw each log lengthwise in appropriate widths until a rough finished slab of lumber was produced. It was a tedious and time-consuming operation, but the labor and saws were plentiful. It was not long before the contractor had an ample supply of crude, green but workable lumber stockpiled for George's purposes.

The next material item would be an integral part of the walls and consisted of full-grown bamboo shoots brought in on overladen oxen-drawn carts. These, in turn, were split into several narrow segments sufficient to be woven into the construction of the inner and outer walls of each building, providing ample installation space between them.

As these phases of the construction process were being carried out, other laborers were busy with their hoe-like tools, digging the foundations at each building site.

Concrete, in Goerig's sense of the word, was not available, as the primary ingredient of cement was impossible to obtain in this sector of China. However, a mixture of lime, water, and miscellaneous filler materials produced a cohesive substance similar to that of concrete.

This composition was then placed in the twelve-by-twelve foundation ditches and eventually formed a solid base for the walls of the buildings. At the same time, vertical eight-foot posts were imbedded at ten-foot intervals to support the horizontal beams for the roof.

Following this phase, a three-foot-high, eight-inches-thick wall consisting of solidly packed earth was tamped into place. Wooden doorjambs and window frames were then strategically located and installed. Then came the double woven bamboo walls, completing the sides of the structures.

Horizontal beams were laid across on the top of the vertical posts to form a ceiling and also the base for the triangular roof. Slats were notched into place from the eaves to the apex of the roof. Carefully hand-placed tile finished off the sloping top.

The final phase consisted of the placing of windows and doors, plastering inside and outside walls, finishing the floors, and general cleanup.

During the period of building construction, Mr. Kao had a separate crew of carpenters busily engaged in the production of the furniture indicated in his original bid. Goerig was amazed at the craftsman's dexterity and workmanship.

Prices on excavation and miscellaneous items were discussed and tentatively agreed upon. Regarding these, Goerig went over to the radio station. After a static-filled conversation with headquarters in Chungking, he received an okay to complete negotiations with the contractor. That evening, he celebrated his business accomplishments by getting "smashed" on puda ju.

George's entertainment was not restricted wholly to drinking. He sought another type of relaxation he had always immensely enjoyed in the past.

"How do you say dollar in Chinese?" Goerig inquired of Lieutenant Lee as a diverse group consisting of himself and five Orientals sat around a covered table in his room playing poker.

"I kinai chien," answered the engineer.

The party of six included George, Captain Ho, Lee, a local banker, and two merchants from Laifeng, whom the private knew only as Loo and Kang. None spoke English, except Lee, who acted as an overall interpreter. As the strange but interesting game progressed, the main topic of conversation centered around the varying amounts shown on the paper money, which spoke for itself.

Soon, the often-repeated words of "open," "laise," "pass," and "out" became common denominators throughout the game.

George had approached Lieutenant Lee a few days previously and suggested that some sort of a card game might be arranged among a few of the select citizens in the community of Laifeng. When he mentioned the word poker, the engineer immediately beamed.

"Poker, oh yes, poker. I played it once or maybe twice in Shanghai. You play?"

"Oh, occasionally," Goerig answered, trying to hide his elation at the possibility of picking up some foreign loose change.

"Tomorrow night, maybe?" Lee responded eagerly.

"Okay by me. It's a deal then. Tomorrow night. I've got the cards."

Lee retorted, "I got the chips."

The unexpected confidence in the Chinaman's voice caused Goerig to hesitate momentarily as he pondered over who was going to teach the other about playing poker.

The conversation had taken place about three weeks previous to a near-tragic incident that unintendedly improved Goerig's meager entertainment situation.

On that night, the private's luck had varied. It had also become more difficult to determine when any of the emotionless faces of his new Chinese friends betrayed the condition of their hands. All of his opponents had learned the art of bluffing to varied degrees and were using it their advantage. However, the game had turned out to be a very pleasant diversion and everyone appeared congenial and happy.

Lieutenant Lee was about to begin a short discourse on the monetary exchange of Chinese to American money when a slight droning sound brought complete silence to the group.

"Japanese plane?" the Chinese officer ventured.

"Be quiet," George ordered as he gestured with his finger over his lips. The muffled noise steadily increased. Finally, Goerig broke the tense suspense.

"Hell, that's no Jap washing machine. It's one of our light bombers. I'll bet it's one of the CACW (Chinese American Composite Wing) B-25s and that he is lost. Let's get our ass in gear."

The private jumped up from the table and the rest of the men followed him out the door. As they reached the exit of the courtyard, he hurriedly turned and hollered to Lieutenant Lee, "Sound the alarm! Get that siren going. Light all those lanterns you have stored for emergencies and pass them out to every man on the base."

Captain Ho needed no interpretation as he was already shouting orders in a high-pitched voice. Soldiers began to materialize out in the open. What appeared to be a mass of confusion suddenly became an orderly formation, as glowing lanterns began being passed out to the sleepy-eyed men.

"Okay, Captain," Goerig shouted and gestured towards the runway, "get them down on the field and you come with me!"

He started the jeep and spun it around as he watched the first line of soldiers disappear over the edge of the bank.

The Chinese officer ran for the moving vehicle and leaped into the rear seat. With a squeal of burning rubber, George headed towards the rutted road and the darkened field. With one hand on the horn, he managed to warn the scurrying soldiers, with their swinging lanterns, to get out of his way. Following several severe jostlings, with the captain anxiously holding on to the bottom of his canvas-covered seat, they managed to reach the airstrip.

Handing Ho a long flashlight powered by six batteries to aid him in the directing of his men, Goerig raced over to the far side of the short runway. Braking the jeep to a stop, he jumped out on the ground and began the disbursement of the soldiers along that side. He watched as the Chinese were being spaced out in an orderly way around the entire perimeter of the airstrip, with the glow from the sputtering wicks acting like so many fireflies dancing in the dark. As soon as the private was convinced he was not needed, he drove back over to join the seemingly calm Chinese officer as he talked with Lieutenant Lee. It appeared they were both eagerly enjoying the responsibility suddenly thrust upon them.

Fortunately, the skies were cloudless. An orange, crescent-shaped halfmoon seemed like a permanent fixture on the darkened background. The complete silence imposed upon the soldiers had an eerie effect on the three men. In their haste to expedite the lighting of the runway, they had all but ignored the original droning sound that had initiated their efforts.

Plaintively, Goerig scanned the endless expanse of space, attempting to sight any tell-tale moving lights. The motor noise had vanished completely.

"Well, all we can do is wait," the private offered with a resigned shrug of his shoulders.

As he turned to get back in his jeep and make himself comfortable, a sudden roar of screaming engines shattered the night's silence. The landing lights of an approaching plane pierced the center of the air strip as it swooped over the small knoll at the near end of the runway. It was a B-25 bomber. Skillfully guiding the twin-motored craft down above the heads of the startled, lantern-bearing soldiers, the pilot made a perfect landing on the hard-packed surface.

"Wonderful," hollered George, "he's going to make it!"

The private gunned his jeep, and with Ho and Lac perilously hanging on to its sides, they bounded down the airstrip after the rolling bomber. With screaming brakes and flaps down, the smell of burning rubber invaded their nostrils. The craft continued its unabated forward motion till mounds of excavated dirt loomed dangerously close ahead.

"What the hell's the matter? Why can't he stop the damn thing? He's going to crack up, sure as hell!" Goerig screamed.

The words had no sooner been uttered when, with a sickening crash, the bomber came to a shuddering halt. George wheeled the jeep up alongside the crippled plane. As the private got out and started towards the battered fuselage, he suddenly stopped. Incredibly, Goerig held up one hand and with the other he pointed to the open bomb-bay doors. All the bombs were still resting snugly in their racks. The three men quickly realized that they all could have easily been blown into eternity. The private's war career had been perilously close to being concluded.

With frightened looks of disbelief, Ho and Lee shook their heads. After a few agonizing moments, a slim, grinning Chinese, dressed in a jump suit, emerged from the plane. He was followed by four visibly shaken Chinese crewmen supporting a fifth whose left leg was dragging on the ground.

"What in God's name are you trying to land a plane full of bombs on this short runway for?" George hollered at the officer. "You must be crazy or something."

Looking quizzically at the private, he then turned to Lieutenant Lee and began what appeared to be some sort of an explanation, accompanied by waving gestures of his hands.

"What the hell is he saying?" George yelled at the engineer.

Lee threw up his hands, his face wearing an expression of futility. "Cannot understand. I believe he speaks Cantonese. It is completely different from Mandarin."

Captain Ho confidently approached the pilot, and after a short monosyllabic conversation with Lee listening attentively, it was determined that the plane's bombardier did not want to waste his bombs over some rice paddy.

Goerig just shook his head. He got back in the jeep followed by Lee and Ho. The pilot and the injured co-pilot shared the rear seat.

"Let's get on the radio and contact the CACW headquarters in Chungking and let them know where some of their wandering boys are tonight."

Maneuvering his vehicle around the crippled plane, their lights picked up the straggling forms of the soldiers as they trudged back up the hill towards the compound. With a roar of the engine, Goerig started tip the bumpy road. As the group pulled into the parking area, the station master hollered for men to help the impaired co-pilot into his office. George and Lee headed for the radio room.

The engineering officer moved into the chair vacated by the night operator and proceeded to try and make contact with the Chungking radio station. After several minutes of garbled sounds and static noises, Lee succeeded and began explain the tragic occurrence of the evening.

After satisfying himself that a proper report about the crash had been made, the private was notified that an investigating team would be sent down in the morning. He returned to his room to get a warmer jacket and figured he would go back and pick up the balance of the crew. His poker friends had all left, but out of idle curiosity he walked over to the table and turned over the last hand he had been dealt. As Goerig looked down at the mocking faces of three kings and two jacks, he muttered to himself,"To hell with those slant-eyed bastards. They just cost me a bundle. Let 'em get back up here on their own."

He pulled back the covers on his bed and decided to call it a night. The last thing he remembered was thinking, "And to think that son of a bitch would rather save his bombs and risk his plane."

The following morning dawned clear and the weather felt crisp. Captain Ho had taken care of the necessary details involved in feeding and bunking down his new unexpected visitors. The language barrier was slowly being overcome, as animated attempts at conversation and wild arm gesturing became a common sight. There seemed to be no despondency on the pilot's part of having cost the United States government approximately a quarter of a million dollars, besides endangering the lives of his own crew plus a score of Chinese soldiers and last but not least George's own life. The private selfishly considered the latter possible casualty as the most important. That's a helluva way he might have died for his country!

The monotonous drone of a C-47's engines announced the arrival of the requested transport. On board was a Captain West and two technical sergeants, who had come to check out any usable parts that could be salvaged from the wrecked plane. They notified Goerig that a jeep and a truck had already left Liangshan with salvage experts to aid in "Operation Vulture." The private later learned that the safe recovery of a top-secret bomb site was their main objective.

Realizing that his entertainment program was at a very low ebb, George approached the salvage captain and bluntly asked him if there was any chance of recovering the plane's radio, which was undamaged aboard the stricken aircraft. The officer didn't see any reason why George couldn't have it since it definitely was not listed as a top-secret mechanism. Later in the day, Goerig drove down to the field and eagerly helped load the receiving set in his jeep. One of the sergeants aided him in getting it set up in his room, and the private found himself in business. Welcome Tokyo Rose and your sentimental recordings from statewide! It proved quite an asset and a morale booster.

Happily, George reflected that the Cantonese pilot wasn't such a bad guy after all.

Construction on the campsite was proceeding in an orderly fashion and work was surprisingly ahead of the schedule that had been worked out by Captain Lewis and himself. The officer had notified George that plans and specifications had been drawn up for the extension and widening of the Laifeng runway and that he should expect visits from some of the contractors, who would be bidding on the project.

CHAPTER TEN

On the morning of March tenth, nineteen hundred and forty-five, there occurred an incident that will always live on as one of the fondest memories of Private Goerig's life.

At approximately 7 am, he was awakened by a terrific din and clamor. Sleepily, he got out of bed, dressed, and looked out the door to see what was causing all the racket. Gathered in the courtyard were Captain Ho, Lieutenant Lee, their families, plus new-found friends from Laifeng and several faces he had never seen before. They were banging on pans, blowing horns, and shooting off firecrackers. George could finally discern that the chorus of shouts consisted of a carefully rehearsed version of "Happy Birthday."

One of the station master's small sons timidly came forward with a courteous bow and held out a silken white banner with red Chinese characters interwoven on the face of the scroll. Lieutenant Lee held up his hand requesting silence. Pointing to the beautifully embroidered work Goerig held in his hand, he made a simple proclamation.

"Mister George," he began, "we all wish you a happy and prosperous birthday on this, your anniversary."

Then, discreetly bringing his other hand from behind his back, he proudly presented the amazed private with a mahogany plaque upon which was a silver facing. Inscribed thereon were the English words, "To George

Goerig on his birthday, March 10, 1945. With many best wishes, Lt, Lee and Capt. Ho."

For one of the few times in his life, Goerig could not find words to express his emotions. Tears started to form in his eyes and roll unabashedly down his cheeks. He finally blurted out, "Thank you all, very, very much!"

George turned and went back into his room. Closing the door, he sat down on his bed with the two presents clasped in his hands. Suddenly, he found he could no longer hold back his feelings and broke into uncontrollable sobbing. It was too beautiful and too wonderful to believe.

A half hour had passed and a knock came on the door. It was Chen. "Breakfast leady," he announced. The private walked, over to let him in. The houseboy had a shining tray in his hands laden with beaming eggs, crisp toast, and bacon. Through the open door, Goerig noticed unusual, bustling activity going on in the courtyard. It seemed as though the area had turned into a virtual beehive.

Tables were rapidly being set up in the open space. The walls were being whitewashed. Flowers from the garden were being cut and bunched.

After eating breakfast, George wandered through the compound. There seemed to be an air of festive gaiety among the bustling personnel. It then occurred to Goerig that perhaps some sort of a party was being prepared in honor of his birthday.

His reasoning was confirmed later. Shortly before midafternoon, a dirt-covered jeep roared up to the compound gates in a whirl of dust. Out climbed Captain Lewis and an enlisted man.

"Are we in time for the party? Just got the news last night in Liangshan and busted our ass getting down here. Happy Birthday, George," he said, laughing.

George thanked the officer, but before he could continue, the latter remarked, "I might give you a bit of warning. A lot of people are going to be toasting you to your health. They use a small teacup and the drink is called *puda ju,* meaning rice wine. It is fermented and is 'dynamite.' They use three different phrases for their toasts. One is *'E din din,'* which means a drop at a time. The second one is *'swebien,'* meaning as much as you like. But the third one is the baby you have to watch. It is called *'gombey,'* and that is bottoms up. They'll do their best to get you loaded, George, since you are the guest of honor. It's just an old Chinese custom regarding Americans. One thing about it, though, is that you'll be eating during this time and the food will usually soften the potency. But it still can knock you off your feet, as I learned the hard way."

The captain then excused himself to get cleaned up and pay his respects to the station master. Goerig reflected momentarily on what his superior had just informed him about, and he quickly decided to go in search for his houseboy, Chen, who he knew would be his personal waiter at the dinner. As he passed the set-up tables, he managed to grab a bottle of the puda ju, which was clear as water, and slip it under his jacket. A devious plan was forming in his mind. Finding the lad by the door of the compound, the private motioned for him to come out by his jeep. Goerig took out the wine bottle and, making sure that nobody was watching, he poured its contents out on the ground. Taking the emergency can of water from the back of the vehicle, George then proceeded to fill the empty bottle. Chen's eyes bulged and a look of horror came over his features. He shook his head. "No, no!" he cried.

"Yes, yes," Goerig sternly replied. "You, my boy. No worry, I'll take care of you." George put his hand on the boy's shoulder to offer reassurance. Finally, Chen calmed down and in a resigned manner managed to display a sickly smile. "Okay, okay," he whispered as though the two were in the midst of a great conspiracy. Actually, he didn't realize what a terrible broach of etiquette his roaster was about to perform. Neither did his master.

As the private walked back into the compound, Lieutenant Lee rushed over and exclaimed, "Mister George, we are looking for you! The basketball game will start soon. You play, won't you?"

"Okay, but I'm not in shape" was the answer. "Don't expect too much. " George walked over to his room to put on a pair of shorts.

The basketball court consisted of hard-packed clay and due to the lack of space was approximately a third smaller than the standard size area. What the players lacked in finesse and adroit ball handling they compensated for with enthusiasm and spirit. Both teams were comprised mostly of the Chinese soldiers on the base. However, Lee and Goerig managed to get into the thick of the action and eventually came out on the winning side. George wouldn't have been too surprised to learn that the final outcome had been "fixed" in his favor. After all, it was his birthday.

Competitive races and individual athletic feats were on the agenda. A small group of spectators provided a lively background for the various events. Finally, a large Chinese gong was sounded. Everybody was informed that dinner was ready.

Goerig was amazed at the assembled personnel gathered around the tables in his honor. There were merchants, bankers, landowners, and even visiting military officers from the neighboring towns. Lieutenant Lee led the host around to each table and introduced him to the various dignitaries. Captain Lewis was called upon to stand up and received a polite ovation. He was content to remain in the background and seemed delighted at the attention that was being lavished upon his protégé.

The first course for dinner consisted of one large baked fish. This was carefully placed in front of George with its head pointed in his direction. He was informed by the Chinese engineer, who was sitting on his right, that this gave the host the unique privilege of eating the head. George politely declined. Lee eagerly accepted Goerig's suggestion that he himself should have the honor.

The various plates of fried chicken, braised beef, curried lamb, assorted green vegetables, and the inevitable bowls of steaming rice were served in an unending stream. As he had been warned, there was also the unending flow of well-wishers, who would continually stop by at George's table to share a toast. The private would normally suggest a *swebien,* but at their insistence he would graciously *"gombey"* them with his watered drink. His houseboy would dutifully refill the small teacup with the water-filled bottle. Occasionally, Lieutenant Lee would glance over at the perfectly sober private amazed at the capacity the host had for the potent liquor.

Finally, after the dinner was half over, the officer beckoned over his shoulder to Chen. With his finger pointed to the bottle the boy held in his hand, Lee indicated that he wanted some of the same poured into his cup. The lad looked at his master pleadingly as a red flush penetrated his yellow, boyish face.

Goerig looked at the lieutenant. The engineer was indeed serious. George resignedly nodded his head and said, "Okay, okay, you win. Pour him a drink, Chen. Gombey, lieutenant, good luck."

As the officer gulped the drink down, he looked at George in disdainful contempt as though he had caught the host cheating at cards. Quickly, the private pleaded with the engineer, "Now, don't blame my boy. He did this on orders from me. I accept full responsibility."

With an embarrassed expression on his face, George looked around at the nearby tables. The sudden silence confirmed his suspicions. They must have overheard the conversation at the table and now were beginning to murmur among themselves. He realized his stupid little scheme had backfired and shortly his deception would become a topic throughout the courtyard.

In no time, he found himself besieged from all sides with toasts of "gombey!" Despite his futile efforts, Goerig began to feel no pain. To make matters worse, he watched as his superior, Captain Lewis, slowly slid under his table. The Americans had managed to lose quite a bit of "face" on that fateful day of March 10th, George's birthday. That puda ju was definitely a powerful drink.

The last thing George remembered was standing at the door of the compound as his guests left. He had been shaking hands with all the men and, despite the efforts of Lieutenant Lee, was trying to kiss the ladies goodnight. He learned later, much to his chagrin, that such was not a normal Chinese custom.

In the morning, a hung over Captain Lewis left for Enshih. Fortunately, his aide was driving.

CHAPTER ELEVEN

Life at the Laifeng air base had settled down into a pleasant routine. Arrangements had been made concerning the hiring of a Chinese staff to take over the menial tasks of kitchen and mess hall operations, plus the general housekeeping of the tents and maintenance of the camp site. Goerig had been notified from Chungking that he could expect the arrival of the first contingent of Air Force personnel at any time. They did arrive on one cloudy afternoon, on schedule.

Two jeeps and four six-by-six GI trucks rolled up, loaded with miscellaneous equipment, parts, and fuel for the expected P-38s. Various essential food provisions and camp necessities were included. Despite the welcome commodities, George was primarily interested in meeting the group of men who accompanied the convoy. He found that they were comprised of a cross section of average GIs and surprisingly seemed to be very content with their surroundings.

The top-ranking non com was a master sergeant by the name of Mike Mulkowski. The man was built like a former All American football player George knew back at the University of Washington. The two were soon to become close friends and the disparity of their ratings created no problem. The sergeant explained that he had been with the Twenty First Reconnaissance Squadron since its inception back in the States.

Mike informed Goerig, "These pilots we have coming in tomorrow are a helluva bunch of good characters. There will be one captain and five lieutenants. Ratings don't mean too much as long as we do our job and keep their planes in good flying condition. They are allergic to crashing up," he said, laughing. "But who isn't? We haven't lost one yet."

George thought to himself, "I only hope that he can say the same thing by the time he's ready to leave Laifeng." Unfortunately, he couldn't.

"If there is anything I can possibly do for you, let me know," Goerig began. "I'll be staying at the Chinese compound. We'll be expecting some new contractors in here very shortly. They will be working on the extension and widening of the existing runway. I'll see to it that they will not be interfering with your operations."

George purposely neglected to inform the Sergeant that there would be approximately thirty thousand Chinese laborers working in the same vicinity. The private did not want him to get unnecessarily upset so soon. One thing at a time, he figured.

"Come on, I'll show you around."

After a brief tour of the camp site, they inspected the newly finished buildings. Mike seemed quite satisfied with the situation. He issued a brief order to one of his men, then he turned towards George.

"We are going to have a fairly large transmitter flown in shortly," he said. "Wonder if we can take a look at your radio shack to check and see if we'll have any trouble moving it in."

"Let's go," the private answered. "No time like the present."

Mulkowski momentarily hesitated. "Wait a minute. As long as we have some spare time on our hands, perhaps I could interest you in a little libation before dinner."

The sergeant had just pleasantly surprised Goerig.

"Why not?" the latter eagerly responded, trying to disguise his eagerness.

Mike walked over to his jeep and began groping into a canvas suit bag. He pulled out a bottle of Scotch, Johnnie Walker no less. "Perhaps we had better go up to your place, so we can have a little privacy. The radio shack can wait."

They jumped into Goerig's jeep and in a very short time the two were sitting at the table in the secluded confines of George's room. "Water or soda?" Goerig asked.

"You have to be kidding. Where the hell do you get soda around here?" the sergeant inquired.

"To tell you the truth, I'm kidding. I don't even have any ice cubes. But if I can stand it, I hope you can."

George poured out two hefty shots of the precious liquid and they leaned back to enjoy the water-chafed drinks. The private then began to realize how much he had missed the delicious, smoky taste of the stateside Scotch. He savored every sip as though it was going out of style.

"Never had it so good. Glad you could make it," Goerig remarked after a short silence.

"So am I, George."

Following the first couple of drinks and a bit of convivial conversation, the two managed to convince themselves that having dinner would probably shatter the euphoria and create an unnecessary interruption to a pleasant social situation. They finished the bottle.

"I'm looking forward to your meeting with my boss, Captain Marsh," Mike said. "I want to see the expression on his face when he learns the top man in charge here has the grand rank of private. It'll make no difference to him, but the meeting should be interesting." The sergeant smiled as he finished his drink.

"Well, Mike," George countered, "Captain Lewis is the real top man in charge. I'm only filling in for him when he's not here. He has two other bases to watch over despite the engineering problems that might arise here. So that puts me fairly well on my own, and I enjoy it."

George explained about his complications in Burma and his close call on the general court martial charge. An hour went by and then, reluctantly, the sergeant rose to his feet.

"Better get down and see how the fellows are making out. They have a lot to do before dark. Have to be ready for our fly boys' arrival tomorrow."

George suggested that he stay and have dinner with him.

Mike shook his head. "I'll take a rain check on that for sure."

The two drove back to the campsite and Goerig informed the master sergeant that he would get in touch with him in the morning.

CHAPTER TWELVE

With their gleaming twin fuselages brilliantly shining in the noonday sun, five P-38s swooped out of the sky over Laifeng and zoomed down a few feet above the airstrip. As if in a courteous salute, they rose and in perfect unison did a complete roll and lazily drifted into a landing formation. George and Captain Ho were in the jeep and down on the runway before the whirling propellers had come to a hesitant stop. Mike and several of his men were already standing by.

The plastic canopies were rolled back and five husky, helmeted pilots emerged from their planes. The one in the lead aircraft briskly strode over to the gathered group and with an acknowledging wave of his arm to Mike, hollered, "Where is all the welcoming committee, Sergeant, and the red carpet?"

Mulkowski laughed. "You are looking at them, Captain. I want you to meet Captain Ho Ka Jan, the Station Master, and Private George Goerig, the top American in charge of construction on this base. George, please meet Captain Marsh, my boss."

The officer stopped and with an incredulous look began to stutter. "Did, did you say Private Goerig?"

George approached, with an outstretched hand, momentarily forgetting the ritual of saluting.

"You heard right, sir. And speaking for Captain Ho and myself, we welcome you to Laifeng."

"But where is your commanding officer?" he asked.

"At the present time, I am in charge of this base," Goerig confidently replied.

"That is good enough for me" was the answer. "Are the planes okay where they are parked now for the time being?"

"Fine, Captain," the private replied. "We'll make arrangements for a permanent location after you get settled down and when we have time to go over future construction plans for the field. I have acquainted Sergeant Mulkowski with your new camp site, and I hope you enjoy the facilities. Please feel free to call on me at any time."

George had started a concluding salute when he was abruptly interrupted by Captain Marsh. "Hold on a minute, none of that army protocol is necessary around here. We've got a lot of work to do. I'll just shake your hand and thank you for the reception. I'm sure that we are all going to get along fine."

═

Things had quieted down a bit after the "recon" outfit had accustomed themselves to the simple life they had to enjoy. There were no movies, no dances, and no girls available. Not even a USO show stopped by. Most of the fellows anxiously awaited a letter from home and then kept busy writing back to their wives and girlfriends in their spare time.

George was pleasantly surprised one afternoon when he received a heavily wrapped package from his hometown. After removing several layers of wrapping paper, he found a laminated wooden shoe box. George tentatively shook the object and was rewarded by gurgling sounds. In frantic anticipation of finding what was inside, he used a heavy hammer to break the box open. His efforts were not in vain when he found himself holding a bottle of Vat 69 in his hands. He hastily searched for the sender's name. It was from Charlie, his good friend in the States. That night was going to be one not to be remembered.

By approximately 9 o'clock, a full moon was rising over the distant hills on the far side of the airfield. The private carefully wrapped his precious bundle of joy in the remnants of an old towel. The compound was especially quiet as Goerig climbed into his jeep and started down the steep hill to the airstrip. Reaching the edge of the runway, he moved out to the center of it and parked.

Gazing up at the starlit sky with emotion, he removed the towel from around the bottle and pulled out the cork. Slowly, he took a sip. Six hours later the sleeping private was awoken by a hand on his shoulder. Someone was trying to arouse him out of his drunken stupor.

"Mistah George, mistah George, you okay?" It was his indispensable houseboy, Chen.

Goerig rose up from his cramped position and shivered. "Where the hell am I?"

His mind was woozy as he tried to regain a semblance of sobriety. An empty bottle slid off his lap to the floor of the jeep. He again shook his head and looked gratefully at the wide-eyed lad. "I'm okay. Get your ass in here and let's get back home."

As he started the engine, George looked over to his servant. "Chen, you are a living doll. Thanks for waking me up."

"Doll. What doll?" Chen asked earnestly.

George gazed at the boy and laughed. Putting his arm around the lad's skinny shoulder, he said, "Some time, some place, you'll find a real doll. Then you will know what I'm talking about."

Chen giggled, not understanding what his master was talking about. Goerig gunned the motor and, with spinning wheels, they climbed back up the hill.

"Thanks, Charlie. I needed that drink."

CHAPTER THIRTEEN

There was one missing factor in Goerig's military life which bothered him. It was the disappointing lack of a normal sexual relationship. He considered himself as a red blooded, able-bodied, normal American man whose natural desires had been unfortunately detoured indirectly by the Air Force Command. Having no other valid excuses, he blamed them for sticking him in a wasteland of unavailable females—Laifeng, China. Realizing his precarious position as the only American representative in the small Chinese district, he was still determined to try and satisfy his sexual needs. What about Helen? Well, of course George thought about his wife and his marriage vows. And of course he felt guilty. But he was also a young man in a war zone with a young man's overwhelming desires. Under normal circumstances, he'd never cheat on Helen, who he loved and respected. These were not, however, normal circumstances. Plus, George was clever, which allowed him to come up with pretty good rationalizations.

One day, he ventured a discussion with Lieutenant Lee regarding the possibilities for meeting young ladies around Laifeng. From all appearances and in accord with the Chinese moral code, he couldn't perceive an illicit affair by chance, but preferred to be introduced to someone. The engineering officer was very sympathetic about the subject, but being such a gracious, understanding host, he told George he would see what could be done about the private's inclinations.

As a week passed, the nightly poker sessions continued. On one certain night, however, the game was interrupted by a timid knock on Goerig's door. An expectant looking Lee hurriedly excused himself and went outside. After a few minutes, he came back in the room and beckoned for George to come join him.

The private has just won a tidy little pot and had thrown his cards in the center of the table. As he picked up his winnings, he pardoned himself and went outside.

The courtyard was dark and Lee was busily engaged in a whispered conversation with an ancient-looking Chinese woman. Standing at her side was a diminutive dark-haired girl with a frightened look on a tear stained face. She shyly hung back from the two bargainers, who were obviously ignoring her. Finally, the Lieutenant motioned for Georg to come over.

"It is all prepared, Mister George, here is the girl we talked about."

Out of the corner of his eye, the private watched as Lee stuffed some bills into the old woman's grasping hands. His emotions became of a mixed nature. However, George quickly overcame his embarrassment at the awkward situation.

Taking the girl by her hand, he led her over to his jeep and gently helped her get inside. She kept her head down as her long black tresses hid her face.

As he started the vehicle and swung it briskly around, George thought he could discern a muffled sobbing. His mind was so engrossed in what he had planned for the evening that he was determined he was not going to be distracted in any way.

A Chinese guard was posted outside the radio shack as Goerig drove up. The private got out and indicated for the man to leave. As the soldier hesitated, George impatiently placed a well-aimed kick in the seat of his pants. He was always led to believe that a good offense was the best defense, or something like that.

Gently guiding the trembling young girl inside the building, he turned to switch on the portable generator. A blinking ceiling light began to glow as Goerig pointed over to the single cot that he had wisely obtained for such an occasion. The girl stood immobilized as George began unbuttoning his shirt. Suddenly, he stopped and slowly walked over to the small, quivering Chinese girl. Raising her drooping chin, Goerig was met by a swollen, wide-eyed, frightened face, whose tears were rolling unceaselessly down her reddened cheeks. George quickly pulled his hand away and swore.

"What the hell are those bastards trying to do? You're barely nothing more than a child."

The angry, sympathetic private took out his handkerchief and tenderly began dabbing at the tears. The intermittent sobs continued to shake her small body as he gently led her out the door.

"Okay, come on, we're getting out of here now."

Silently, he cussed his lieutenant friend as they drove back down to the compound. Upon reaching the gates, Goerig helped the still-trembling girl out. Thrusting some Chinese notes in her hands, he kissed her lightly on the cheek and indicated for her to stay by the jeep while he went inside to get her mother. Could such a callous woman possibly be this helpless child's mother? The private shook his head and wondered.

As George started for the entrance, the scared girl suddenly turned and fled. He puttered to himself, "Never again" as he slowly walked back to his room and told himself that he had definitely had it.

CHAPTER FOURTEEN

The American system of sealed bids to determine the low bidder on a contract was the standard, fair method used by the Air Force engineers when dealing with the Chinese contractors. However, Private Goerig's personal experience regarding such matters in Laifeng would prove very disappointing. Four contractors had submitted their bids on the extension and widening of the projected runway. They were all from Chungking and unintentionally seemed to comprise a close-knit group. This was definitely indicated by an incident shortly after the award of the contract to the lowest bidder.

The contract was in excess of three million dollars, American currency. Representatives of the four companies were present at the meeting in Laifeng called by Lewis. Discussions were primarily with Chiang Tai, the low bidder. However, it became very apparent that all four of the competitors were going to have an equal share of the future work, eventually splitting up the construction of the air strip into four equal sections.

George looked at his Captain in surprised amazement.

"We have a word for that back in the States, sir, don't we? I believe it is called collusion, or price fixing. Whatever."

He nodded his head and shrugged his shoulders. Rising from the table, the captain formally announced, "Well, gentlemen, I guess your decision brings this meeting to a close. We'll expect work to start within the week. Good day."

The two Americans walked back to Goerig's room. The captain glowered at his aide. "Okay, so what the hell can we do about it? We still take orders and one of them is to get this project done. We figured out ourselves that the total cost will not be more than one million dollars. But what can we do? So they make a killing out of Uncle Sugar while we're over here saving their asses from the Japs. A good portion of those profits will find its way back into the silk lined pockets of Chiang Kai-Shek and his corrupt mob of organized Oriental gangsters."

Smashing his fist into the open palm of his other hand, he continued, "If I had my way, we'd all get the hell out of here and let the Nips take over. The Kuomintang regime is rotten to the core."

Having momentarily expressed his sincere, hidden feelings, the captain got up from the table and went over to the runway construction plans taped on the side wall. He started in to explain, "With all those slant-eyed bastards working all over this runway, we are going to have a time keeping an area clear for the 'recon' outfit. We might have to have Captain Ho use some of his boys to keep that existing runway clear. I'll leave that up to you."

"Thanks a lot," George replied sarcastically. "I'll do something for you sometime."

"Well, you have to earn your pay someway or other, don't you?"

"Okay, okay, since I have found out I can't take it out in trade, I guess the money will have to suffice."

Hesitantly, he then told his superior about his encounter with one of the local juveniles and how sexual deprivation was making him demoralized.

Lewis looked at his aide momentarily, then answered, "George, Laifeng is not the only place in China. When I go back to headquarters in Chungking, I'll inform your enlisted engineering comrades about your frustrated life down here. According to the rumors up at the main base, it seems that the boys have an interesting sex orgy at least once a month in their barracks room. I understand that the local contractors furnish the stateside booze and the girls. The doors are then locked and I guess anything goes.

"You are due for a week's vacation and I'll see that you get it. The next time I come down, I'll bring somebody to relieve you for the time. I think you'll like Chungking. You'll meet some nice fellows up there."

George perked up. "To hell with the fellows, I want to meet some dames. I hope you're not kidding me, captain—are you?"

"No, kid, I'm not," he replied. "Let's say in a couple of weeks or so. Okay?"

"Beautiful, I'll have this job in top shape when you come down. You won't have a thing to worry about. I'll manage to keep the runway clear for the 'recon' boys to keep busy with no interference."

Lewis laughed. "Hell, I know you'll handle that, George. I'm only worrying about the gals in Chungking. Okay, now let's get back to business and figure out how we are going to net up this operation."

The next several hours were involved in working out a feasible progress schedule for the completion of the entire project, plus the time elements required for each phase. A deadline had to be set for the final date when the Fourteenth Air Force could officially move in with their fighter planes. Also, the manner of making payments to the contractor regarding the unit prices on the job was discussed. Finally, the captain stood up.

"The way the war is going, it might just be all over before this job is completed. I think that headquarters will determine the way in which payments will be made. But if I was a betting man, I'd say those bastards will wind up with the whole kit and caboodle, whether they finish the work or not. There is nothing we can do about the damn thing, so why worry?"

With a wave of his hand, he indicated the matter was closed and abruptly changed the subject. "How about these poker games you've been telling me about? Is there any easy money to be got? I'm ready."

That night the captain was relaxed and at ease. He and George had had several puda jus mixed with canned grapefruit juice, their favorite cocktail before and after dinner.

As the poker game progressed, Lewis would raise, bluff, and seldom pass. Despite a continuance of poor hands, his newfound Chinese friends would usually toss in their cards and then shake their heads at the captain's poker skills. It soon became obvious to George that they were in favor of having his superior leave the game a happy man. The night was a terrific success.

The following morning, after a brief tour of the campsite and the airfield, Lewis bid Goerig a fond farewell.

"Don't forget, George, within two weeks, Chungking, I promise."

The private waved and shouted, "I'll be waiting, sir!"

CHAPTER FIFTEEN

For the extension and widening of the Laifeng Air Base, the Chinese laborers had moved in on the job like so many ants. Goerig didn't know where they came from and couldn't have cared less. However, the mass of humanity was comprised of over thirty thousand human beings. Despite the great number of coolies involved, the general organization and the orderly placement of the laborers were hard to believe.

It seemed to Goerig that the logistics of preparing to feed and sleep such a vast multitude of people in such a short period of time would be a tremendous task. However, he had not reckoned with the simple needs necessary to accommodate such a crowd. Actually, everything seemed to run rather smoothly.

At first, the private was slightly awed by the great responsibility he had assumed. As time progressed, however, Goerig's confidence in his own abilities grew, and he soon had the respect of the engineers and contractors alikc.

The Chinese system of operations for general construction work was broken down into several phases corresponding to different aspects of the project.

Excavation of the ground was the initial project. One group of men would hack away at the packed earth, leveling the high ground with hoe-like tools. The excavated material was then thrown into weaved baskets hung on the ends of a bamboo rod balanced over the shoulders of other coolies. These hurriedly followed a lead man for disposal in designated low areas.

Secondly, huge solid stone rollers, weighing in excess of ten tons, were pulled by three to four hundred laborers straining at the yokes embedded in their sunken shoulders. Their only diversion they was when one of their crew would slip and fall, only to be crushed by the oncoming roller. Work would temporarily stop as the majority of the Chinese would go back to enjoy the final agonizing writhings of their fallen comrade.

The next step involved the rock collecting. Imported coke-burning trucks hauled various-size boulders down from the neighboring countryside and dumped them on the airstrip. Mounded graves were stripped of any semblance of material that could be used in the final rock surfacing. Gravel from the nearby riverbed was loaded and hauled in the customary baskets and hastily unburdened in calculated piles.

The next step, which was really incredible, involved small family groups usually comprised of several generations sitting in a circle around a cluster of boulders with small hammers in their hands, breaking up the rocks into suitable crushed sizes. Goerig was amazed at the results of these primitive construction methods.

The final phase in the operation was the spreading of the crushed rock with a blend of lime and water interspersed over the entire area. After one more final rolling, that portion of the project was completed.

Three weeks had passed since Captain Lewis had departed for Chungking. Despite the fact that Goerig had become completely engrossed in the engineering and construction activities that had been left in his hands, he still dreamt about his future trip to Chungking. As time went by, he was getting more impatient and worried. Finally, during the heat of one mid-afternoon, a cloud of dust rapidly approaching the runway announced the arrival of his superior.

Captain Lewis, accompanied by two dust-covered, disheveled soldiers, eagerly jumped out of the still running jeep, and said, "Well, damn it, smile, I told you I'd get back here eventually, didn't I?"

"You said two weeks, not three," the private hollered back at him.

"Don't worry," he answered, "Chungking will still be there when you get ready to go. How is the job coming along?"

Without waiting for a reply, he glanced over his shoulder and beckoned to the two sergeants standing behind him. "Come here, damn it, and meet the private who's been running this whole operation. George, this is Frank and Art. They will help out here while you are on your vacation. Now you can grab the next transport to Chungking. I'll give you one week and then you get your ass back here. Okay?"

Slightly dazed by the long-awaited tidings, the private could only meekly answer, "Yes sir."

CHAPTER SIXTEEN

Goerig's only two uniforms had been cleaned, and his shoes had been shined by indispensable houseboy Chen until they glistened. A seldom used tie was uncomfortably knotted in place. George was impatiently waiting by the side of his jeep as the C-47 transport emerged over the knoll approaching the runway. The captain was at his side.

After a perfect landing, the plane suddenly swerved to its right and headed for the drainage ditch adjacent to the airstrip.

"Oh my God, please, not again, not now," George prayed.

Finally, the so-called indestructible "workhorse" of the Air Force came to a leaning stop over the V-shaped channel.

Captain Lewis calmly turned to the sergeant standing behind him. "Get your ass up there to the camp and have all the trucks come down here right now. Get going."

The two then headed for the disabled plane. By the time they had pulled up alongside of it, the pilot had jumped out and was examining the precarious situation. He casually announced, "Guess the brakes locked. Everything seems to be okay, though." He looked around. "Got anything to pull us out of here? If you do, we'll be on our way."

His nonchalance concerning the condition of his plane astounded George; however, it only reaffirmed the terrific confidence which the Air

Force had in the ability of this special breed of airmen in the so-called primitive sectors of China.

Shortly, four trucks appeared on the scene. Tow ropes were securely attached to the plane's landing gear. At a signal from the pilot in the cockpit, the lines tightened and the transport slowly moved forward until it was safely sitting on the hard-packed surfacing of the runway.

With a wide grin on his face, the flying officer jumped down from the side door and ran over to Captain Lewis.

"Thanks a million. Now where is the gent we are supposed to pick up?"

He acted like nothing had ever happened out of the ordinary. Goerig confidently climbed aboard. Exultantly, he said to himself. "Chungking, here I come."

The trip to the temporary capital of China was uneventful. In anticipation of the short vacation that awaited him, George thought that the pounding of his heart would drown out the noise of the rhythmic throb of the engines.

As the C-47 sat down for a perfect landing at the airport and taxied over to its allocated parking space, a topless jeep came roaring up and slid to a tire-burning stop by the side of the transport. While Goerig was stepping down from the aircraft, the two occupants of the jeep rushed over with welcoming smiles.

Simultaneously, they greeted the private.

"We hope you are Goerig, right?"

"Right" was the answer.

"Welcome to Chungking. I'm Bob and this is Dale. Your boss, Captain Lewis, told us to be sure and show you a good time on your vacation." He smilingly laughed, bowed, and added, "Private Goerig, we are at your service. We've all heard about your lousy deal in Burma and maybe we can start making up for that tonight. In our own way, that is."

His buddy, Dale nudged him. "Sometimes you talk too much. Let's get the show on the road."

Throwing the barracks bag over his shoulder, Goerig climbed into the jeep after the others. With a screeching of the tires and smell of burning rubber, the trio was off. George had arrived.

The barracks that housed the enlisted members of the Fourteenth Air Force Engineers measured about thirty by sixty feet. Bunks were set up against the wall. A latrine and showers were conveniently located adjacent to the room. George nodded his head in approval as Dale came up behind him.

"Goerig, you are looking at the best den of iniquity in all of China. I hope you enjoy it."

Trying to suppress his sudden sexual arousal, the private stupidly asked, "But where are the girls?"

Bob laughed. "These are working hours. When nighttime arrives, you are going to be the guest of honor at one of our better orgies. You'd never believe how delightful they are unless you were a part of one."

For one of the few times in his life Goerig stuttered. "But, but how the hell do you get away with it? This is an Air Force base isn't it?"

George's two new friends looked at each other and chuckled. Finally, Dale explained, "Buddy, the engineers run this base, lock, stock, and barrel. If anyone wants something done around here, they have to come to us. Naturally, we are cooperative, and as a result, we usually get to do what we want, with little interference."

Goerig shook his head in feigned disbelief. "Man, if you say so, I'm all for it." Eagerly he asked, "When does the party start?"

Bob quickly filled him in. "The girls get here about eight o'clock. Most of them come from Chungking. We have arrangements with our conniving Chinese contractors to get them here and arrange to take them home when the party is over. Oh," he paused and added, "they also furnish all the booze. Can you imagine a pint of Old Crow costing eighty dollars? We get it for free. All we need for the parties. Uncle Sam is being stuck good by these bastards, so why shouldn't they be nice to us?"

Recalling his own recent experience in Laifeng, Goerig smiled. "Why not? I'm all for it. But eighty bucks for a pint of Old Crow? That sounds real ridiculous. However, if it's free, I'll drink up."

Dale impatiently interrupted the conversation. "Come on, let's break it up. I've got to take George into town. He has to meet his date for the party. Ready, boy?"

George was eager. "Any time you are. Let's be on our way."

The two American engineers found an empty booth in the crowded cafe where Goerig was to be introduced to his prospective date for the evening. The place was humming with activity and crowded with a mixed group of young Orientals and GIs from the airbase. They all appeared to be enjoying themselves.

Dale began telling his guest about the girl he was about to meet and her tragic background. It seemed her parents had been killed in one of the countless indiscriminate Japanese bombings. An American consul and his wife had taken her into their home. After that, she had attended an American school in the city. At the present time, she was living with her grandparents and trying to forget the nightmarish events that had made such an imprint on her young mind. Suddenly, he glanced over at the main door. A short, vivacious, laughing young Chinese girl had just entered. She was immediately surrounded by some of the people standing close by.

"Hey, Susy, over here!" hollered Dale as he waved his arm.

She turned her head and waved back. After a few minutes of animated conversations with several of her friends, she managed to finally get over to the table.

With a mischievous twinkle in her dark, brown eyes, and a disarming smile on her inviting lips she frankly remarked, "Hi, you must be George."

Trying to be very casual despite the rising emotions in his body, Goerig answered, "And you must be Susy. Won't you join us? I've heard a lot about you."

Looking questioning at Dale, she winked and said, "It had better be good."

The girl was wearing a jade green dress slit up one side in the customary Chinese fashion. As she sat down, George couldn't help but notice a beautiful tanned and shapely leg, which he quickly realized was only a small portion of her perfect anatomy. Two small but very tantalizing breasts above a very trim waistline completed the tempting figure and left the private speechless.

Susy and Dale meanwhile were carrying on a lively conversation until the sergeant glanced over noticing his guest's preoccupied attention with the girl's charms.

"Hey, boy, are you still with us? Susy thinks she would enjoy being your date at the party. How about it?"

Dazedly, George glanced up at the vivacious, smiling face.

"I'd love it, when do we start?"

CHAPTER SEVENTEEN

The record player was spinning a new tune that was fast becoming a favorite of everybody. It was, "Cocktails for Two Hic, Hic—Hic," by Spike Jones. A few hours earlier, George had had the opportunity to meet the rest of his temporary roommates and found them all, in his opinion, to be real nice guys. They were all aware of his past and present situations. He was the guest of honor and nothing seemed to be too good for Private Goerig.

Suddenly, he looked up as a bevy of young and gorgeous Chinese girls walked into the room. Immediately spotting Suzy, George waved to her. She quickly smiled, walked over to his table, and sat down.

As the evening progressed, Goerig soon learned that his date was a very accomplished dancer. It had been quite a long time since he had been on a dance floor, but it didn't take long before he was recalling some of the dance steps he thought would be a thing of the past. The free-flowing liquor gave him a warm and glowing sensation. Suzy seemed to be enjoying herself tremendously. They were engrossed in conversation when Bob, who was sitting across their table, stood up and calmly announced, "Well, let's get the ball rolling." With this, he reached behind the back of the girl sitting next to him and subtly unzipped her mandarin dress.

A quick silence came over the expectant group. The girl, in turn, nonchalantly rose from her chair and accommodatingly let the garment fall to the floor. She was very naked with the exception of a small pair of lace panties, barely hiding the dark triangle between her youthful legs. Proudly displaying her protruding charms, she turned towards Bob. Slightly opening her red, moist lips, the girl gently placed her outstretched arms around his neck and slowly drew him to her.

It was then that all hell seemed to break loose.

George unconsciously dropped his arm from around Suzy as he stared, fascinated, at the orgy that was beginning to take place before his startled eyes. The young Chinese maidens were being quickly divested of their meager dresses. In some cases, they were often helping the fumbling hands of some inexperienced engineers who had probably spent too much time over a drafting table and not enough time between the sheets.

Within a few minutes, the lights had been dimmed and the naked, entwined couples were warmly occupying the waiting bunks conveniently spaced around the darkened room. George watched Dale as the latter gently picked up his unresisting date, carried her over to his own cot, and tenderly lay her down. He then knelt down beside her and began kissing her sensuous and luxurious body. The girl began softly moaning and twisting her shapely figure in mounting ecstasy. Finally, unable to wait any longer, she eagerly pulled Dale on top of her.

It was then that George felt a twisting pinch on his arm. He turned his head, still dazed by all the sexual activity being performed about him. He had become completely oblivious to his date.

Suzy was looking at him with disappointed eyes. "Well, don't you remember me? I'm supposed to be your girl for tonight."

Slowly, George's senses began to return to normal as he foolishly asked, "Where do we start?"

The girl's mouth fell open and a disbelieving look came over her young, puzzled face. She hesitantly replied, "Well we could take a shower together." And after a pause, she added, "To start with."

George hastily downed the double bourbon in front of him and reached for the waiting girl's hand. They walked over to the closed cubicle next to the shower. Suzy obligingly turned her back to him. He slowly pulled the dipper of her dress down with trembling fingers and removed the garment from her shoulders. It fell to the floor. She then reached behind her back and unclasped brassier hooks. Bending down, the flimsy piece of lace followed the dress. Without pausing, the girl then enticingly pushed her pink, silk panties down the length of her shapely legs.

George had taken off his shoes as Suzy slowly and tantalizingly turned toward him. He couldn't believe that this provocative, firm body was so close to his. The proud, tender breasts were flawless. The tense, rigid tips were slowly rising as he bent to kiss them. Unexpectedly, she gently covered his mouth with her hand. "Please, not yet. Let me undress you first."

Methodically, she unbuttoned his shirt and then unbuckled the belt. With her nimble fingers, she carefully removed all of his clothing. George stood naked before her. Taking him by the hand, she guided the slightly confused private to the shower stall and turned on the knob. As the water cascaded over the both of them, George took her in his arms and tenderly kissed her. He then took the bar of soap and began massaging her soft, warm, yielding body.

"Why the hell couldn't you have hung your shingle in Laifeng?" he whispered in Suzy's ear.

She bent her head back and looked up at him quizzically. "Shingle? What do you mean by shingle?"

At that moment Goerig had no appropriate answer.

The balance of the week flow by. George's new engineering friend, Dale, through devious means, had managed to commandeer a jeep from the motor pool, and the two were in business. Since the airbase was located a few miles from Chungking, it was imperative to have accessible means of transportation on hand. When Bob could get away, he would join them and they would all go to the big city on a sightseeing tour.

The ravages and desolation of earlier Japanese bombings had left an indelible scar over the entire area, leaving many thousands homeless and an untold number dead. Fortunately, the Flying Tigers had been able to repulse a large portion of the bombers and now, under the new name of the Fourteenth Air Force, was beginning to inflict heavy damage to the enemy air bases and supply lines. Chungking no longer had to worry about future raids.

After a couple of nights at the base and spending a jovial time with his new drinking friends, Goerig broached the subject of possibly seeing Suzy again and taking her out to dinner in the big city.

"George," Dale began, "unless you are loaded with dough, forget it. Those Chink bastards will hook you good." He paused a moment and then reflected. "But, hell, we can go into town and pick her up and bring her back here to the NCO club."

"Hey, wait a minute," Goerig interrupted. "Don't forget your buddy is still a lowly private and I think that perhaps some of your fellow sergeants would frown on that."

"Yeah," agreed Bob. "I keep forgetting about that little technicality of you have such an inconspicuous ranking." He laughed. "But I do know of a small village south of here a few miles where we can get some damn good Chinese chow, and the price is fairly reasonable. Personally, I wouldn't touch that gut-burning fire water, *puda ju,* but let's give it a try anyway."

The three quickly and unanimously agreed. Shortly, arrangements were made and the men were to pick up the girls around six o'clock. However, as George and Dale were getting ready to leave, a sad and dejected-looking Bob walked over to the jeep. "Of all the tough breaks, I forgot that I have duty tonight. You'll have to go on without me. Have fun and a drink on me."

The evening turned into a terrific success. The secluded, warm atmosphere of the small cafe produced a romantic background for the enjoyable foursome. As they drove back towards Chungking, George rode in the back seat with Suzy closely cuddled in his arms. After a short period of silence, the private expectantly asked, "Where now, Dale? You have anything in mind?"

"Yeah," came the answer. "I've definitely got something in mind, but where?"

A small voice piped up. "Why not my place? It's not too far." Suzy had raised her pert little head off Goerig's shoulder, and with a mischievous smile on her lips, waited for an answer. It came fast.

"Just show me where you live, baby!" shouted Dale.

After a half hour's drive and carefully following Suzy's directions, the four pulled up in front of an ancient dwelling that had fortunately been spared from the repeated bombing raids.

Suzy stepped out from the jeep and motioned for the others to follow her. It was getting late and Goerig began wondering who they might meet at that hour of the night in her home. Nobody, he hoped—but he was mistaken.

As they walked into the living room, an elderly couple was sitting at a table drinking tea. Suzy waved a greeting to them and turned. Casually, she explained that they were her grandparents and did not speak English.

"Let's go upstairs." She gestured toward a ladder leading to a trap door in the ceiling. With a shrug of his shoulders, George replied, "Why not?"

The three of them followed Suzy up the ladder into a candle-lit attic. Over at one side, there was a dresser and a double bed. A frayed rug covered the wooden floor. Dale made a leap for the bed with his date in tow.

"First come, first serve," he laughed.

"Hey, wait a minute, to hell with that. We flip a coin, tails or heads?"

"Okay, okay, that's fair enough. But if you win, we take turns. Once on the bed and once on the floor, or vice versa, ol' buddy."

Dale won the toss of the coin. George turned to Suzy and suggested they make themselves comfortable on the floor.

She giggled, walked over to the corner of the room, and pulled out a beaten up mattress. She looked at George with quizzical eyes. "Okay, master?"

He grabbed her in his arms and kissed her moist lips. The candle was blown out and he shortly found his hands again caressing the inviting body he was getting to know better. He whispered again in her ear, "Let them have the damn bed. I'm happy, how about you?"

She drew back and playfully moved her fingers across his chest. Then with a wistful look, she whispered back, "I think I like you, George."

He pulled her back close to him and murmured, "You had better, baby. Cause it's going to be a long night."

She snuggled closer. The rhythmic sound of the creaking bed springs soon lulled them both to sleep.

═

"Larry, get your fanny out of bed. It's seven o'clock. You have to be at the base in one hour."

Goerig's sudden announcement didn't seem to have any effect on the entwined bodies on the bed.

Finally, a muffled voice answered, "So what? They can't fire me, can they?"

George turned back to the sleeping doll in his arms. "Suzy, honey, don't you have to get to work?"

The closed lids of two brown eyes opened slightly and then closed again. "I don't care if I ever go back to work again." She wrapped an arm around her new bed mate. "Kiss me, damn it," she demanded.

Obligingly, George tenderly covered her puckered lips with his own. Suddenly she jumped up. "What time did you say it was? I have to be at work in an hour. As you Americans say, let's get the show on the road."

Quickly, she pecked at Goerig's cheek and bounced up from the mattress. She hastily threw a robe around her shoulders and began climbing down the ladder.

Dale and his friend gathered up their clothes and dressed quickly as George frantically searched for one missing shoe.

═

The whirlwind vacation was over too soon, as Bob and Dale drove their new private friend over to the waiting transport.

"When the hell are you coming back? That was the best party we've had since we first got into this damn country," Dale remarked.

After climbing out of the jeep, Goerig walked over to the door of the waiting plane. Bob was carrying his barracks bag.

"I'll never forget you guys for what you did for me," he started to say. "In fact, your whole bunch has been great to me. Be sure and give them my thanks when you get back. Oh, by the way, you might also thank those Chinese contractors who put on the party."

"Screw those bastards," Dale sneered. "They are probably trying to figure out some angle to get paid back, and they'll think of something."

The same pilot who had flown George up from Laifeng was checking with a mechanic by the fuselage. He looked up as George approached. "Well, how was Chungking? Did your friends show you a good time?"

"You bet they did, sir. Wonderful," he replied.

The pilot laughed. "I'll bet they did, too. Hop aboard, we'll be on our way shortly."

Goerig turned back to his newly found friends and shook their hands. "Thanks again."

Throwing the bag over his shoulder, he climbed aboard the idling aircraft. With a final wave of his hand, he ducked his head and began picking his way by the bucket seats to find a suitable place with an unobstructed view. Finally, he sat down.

As the C-47 circled over the ravaged city and headed East, George locked down and murmured to himself.

"Thanks, Suzy. I needed that."

CHAPTER EIGHTEEN

Life is cheap in China. That is perhaps the greatest understatement that could be made about a human being's existence in that Asian country, where at one time their exquisite culture was unrivaled throughout the world. Goerig had witnessed many shocking incidents that were so commonplace to the Chinese that he knew he could never accept their way of life.

One day, a certain incident occurred that he would never forget. Occasionally, when the private took his jeep on trips down to the airfield and the campsite, he would allow Chang, one of his houseboys, to take over the wheel. Eventually the lad became slightly adept at the art of driving.

One morning Goerig arose, washed, shaved, and set out for an active day of inspection. As he walked over to the location where he normally parked his vehicle in the evening, he found no jeep. Wondering what the hell could have happened, he decided to check in with Captain Ho and Lieutenant Lee. After they had come out of their office and searched around the area, neither was able to give the private an explanation as to what had happened to his only means of transportation.

As they were discussing the situation, the missing jeep came swerving around the corner of the compound. With a grinning, triumphant look on his face, Chang pulled up to a stop and climbed out. An immediate confrontation between the boy and his superiors ensued.

Captain Ho angrily barked out an order to several of the soldiers working in the vicinity. Before George realized what was happening, his houseboy had had his arms trussed behind his back and was being roughly shoved out of the compound.

Goerig looked at Lee and hesitatingly asked, "What are they planning on doing with him?"

His answer was quick and definite. "He is to be shot, now."

"Wait a minute! What did you say?" George hollered.

"He is to be shot," answered the impassive-looking lieutenant.

In total disbelief, the private managed to stutter, "But, but, he was only having a little fun. No harm was done. You can't possibly kill a man for that."

The engineer, his features set in a hard, stubborn manner replied, "I'm sorry if this matter offends you, Mister George. However, Chang has disgraced all of us with his behavior. He does not deserve to live."

Realizing the sudden seriousness of the situation, George became angry. "If you shoot that boy, I will report this incident to my superiors. Under the circumstances, I am the one to decide what to do with him. Right now, I'm asking you to release him. You can do anything you want to him, within reason, but you will not shoot him. With all due respect to your authority and military regulations, I ask you to spare his life."

The two Chinese officers looked at George with disbelieving eyes. They then quickly conferred, and the engineer turned to the American. "As you wish, Mister George. He will not be shot. He will, however, be punished in another manner."

Thanking the both of them, Goerig went back to his room. He began wondering what the other punishment would consist of. He thought to himself, "Oh well, at least he'll still be alive."

That same evening, George had just returned from the airfield and was met at the entrance to the compound by two of his poker-playing friends from Laifeng. They were holding a bird cage, a tethered fowl, and a folded animal skin. Lieutenant Lee was with them as they approached the jeep.

"Mister George," he began, "your friends Mister Soo and Mister Yang have brought you some presents that they thought you might like." Presenting Goerig with a spotted leopard skin, he proudly announced, "This is from one of the few leopards ever found in this area."

Turning to his friends, he picked up the cage. Immediately a wildly chattering bird inside began making strange sounds with a Chinese accent.

"Perhaps, you are more familiar with a bird called a parrot in your country, one that talks. However, this is a Mynah bird, and we hope it can imitate the English language. It is very smart."

Unwrapping a cloth from around the tethered large bird he held in his hands, Mr. Soo dropped it to the ground. It was the most elegant pheasant George had ever seen. Its feathers were a beautiful assortment of various colors. Strutting like a vain peacock, it was restrained only by the leather thong tied around one of its legs.

Goerig profusely thanked his visitors while Lee continued, "These generous men also will provide a pen for the large bird, and it will be placed in the compound by your room."

During the ensuing weeks, the Mynah bird became a very interesting companion to George, while the pheasant remained outside. Uncertain of its sex, he figured it might as well be a female and christened her, Nina. He hung her cage from a beam in the middle of his room since Lee had warned him it would be fair game for any predatory rodents.

In trying to teach Nina how to mimic like a parrot should, Goerig would keep repeating over and over to her such phrases as, "How are you?" "I am fine." "Close the door." The private had difficulty in having the bird say, "Where is my damn supper?" Instead, he decided he had better keep his animated little bird well fed.

George soon found out what an extremely smart student he had on his hands. His affection for his feathered friend increased daily. One night, however, he lowered the cage down and placed it on his table. Goerig was away listening to Tokyo Rose and her American records on his B-25 radio while Nina pushed her beak through the pencil-like bars and bit on a piece of lettuce which was being fed to her. Drowsiness finally got the best of George and he rolled into bed, forgetting to hang the cage back up from the ceiling beam.

The following morning when the private awoke, he glanced over at the cage. Excitedly, he jumped to his feet. The small door of the cage was wide open and his beautiful bird was gone. The multitude of feathers on the floor of the cage indicated that she had put up quite a struggle before succumbing to her attacker. Goerig swore, "That dirty little bastard!" Then he hurled the empty cage against the wall.

Sitting back down on the edge of his bed, he couldn't understand how he wasn't awakened by the noise the Mynah bird must have made during its last moments. Then, slowly he glanced over to the empty bottle of puda ju sitting on the table; it was apparent that he had passed out before returning the cage to its safety under the ceiling beam.

"Never again." He realized that he had previously repeated a similar phrase not long ago. "I guess my luck with females in China has run out. However, Chungking hadn't been too bad. I guess you can't win them all."

George got up, washed, and dressed. Going out into the bright sunshine, he blinked his eyes as he walked over to the pen that had housed his beautiful proud pheasant. He noticed that it no longer had the jaunty strut of a peacock, which it previously had had. It had grown thinner and lost quite a few of its luxurious feathers. At this rate, George thought the bird was not going to last long. He hollered to Chen, who was coming over to feed the gaunt-looking bird.

"Forget it, he won't eat. Get a sack. We're going to take him back to the hills before he dies on us."

They were soon in the jeep, headed for the countryside. After a bumpy ride, Goerig pulled over to the side of the road. "Okay, let it out."

Chen opened the bag, and a frightened but still-agile pheasant flew down to a green pasture. It hesitatingly looked back and then in disbelief at its sudden freedom, bolted through the tall grass.

"Well, that takes care of my bird collection," the private remarked sadly.

With a resigned shake of his head, he turned the jeep around. Chen grinned and with his arm in the air, the extended thumb was waving wildly. "Ding hao, ding hao!" he shouted.

George guessed his Chinese boy had a few humanitarian feelings similar to his own. They roared down the road to the compound, both realizing a fresh feeling of relief and satisfaction.

CHAPTER NINETEEN

The captain and George were driving through the grassy area adjacent to the existing runway. It had started to rain slightly, so they stopped and raised the canvas roof over the jeep, snapping it into place. Suddenly, a shot rang out and the sound reverberated across the valley.

"Oh my God, look, someone has been hit!" Goerig yelled and pointed toward a group of several Chinese peasants running toward one of their companions who was bent over holding on to his leg. The two jumped back in the jeep and raced over to the excited gathering. Sliding to a stop, they leaped out and ran over to the injured man.

Blood was streaming down his leg from a gash above his knee. He was futilely trying to stop the spreading flow. Captain Lewis quickly took off his belt and used it as a tourniquet above the ragged wound.

One of the peasants was chattering excitedly to the others and gesturing wildly with a pointed finger up towards the campsite. Looking up, the two Americans could see nobody. A grim look came over the captain's face while he softly swore. "Some son of a bitch is going to pay for this."

Together they picked the man up and placed him in the back seat as a small mongrel dog started nipping at George's boot. He shook him off, and they got in the jeep. The spinning wheels on the wet ground gradually took hold and they lurched ahead towards the compound.

"You still got that first aid kit in your room?" the captain hollered over the roar of the motor.

George nodded his head as he held his arm around the moaning Chinese to try and steady him. With the other hand, he clasped the temporary tourniquet. They drove up to the portal of the compound and helped the injured man out. He looked pleadingly at the American as Captain Ho came running over to the jeep with Chen following close behind him.

George motioned for his houseboy to help get the peasant to his room. Slipping their arms around his back, the two managed to help him hobble over to the door and sit down on the spare cot.

Goerig went to the wall, took down the large first aid kit off its hanger, and brought it over to the table. In the meantime, Captain Ho, knife in one hand, was cutting off the blood-soaked pant leg, exposing an ugly gash across the front of the man's leg. Chen stood beside his captain with a wash basin of boiled water and a towel. Ho quickly began washing off the wound as George handed him the pack of sulfa from the kit.

The small package was broken open and its contents were liberally sprinkled on the bleeding wound. A compressed bandage was placed over it and a wide strip of gauze was neatly wrapped around the leg. During this process, Chen applied a cold wet towel to the patient's perspiring forehead as he nodded his head in thanks.

Lieutenant Lee had just arrived on the scene, and after being briefed on what had happened, turned to Captain Lewis.

"I'll take care of him now and see that he gets home alright. We'll also see that he gets proper attention till the wound heals. Thank you, Captain."

Lewis started for the door, his face a livid red.

"Come on, Goerig, we're going to find out who that son of bitch is who likes to play with guns."

George hurried after him. The rain had started to fall in earnest, and he knew a storm was brewing. However, he didn't realize it would be nothing compared to the one that was gathering momentum in front of himself. As Lewis jumped in the jeep, he pressed down on the starter, and the engine responded immediately as if it knew the captain wanted to go someplace in a hurry. The private grabbed on to the side and leaped into the rear seat.

"God help someone," he prayed.

Captain Lewis had already started up the walk to the squadron headquarters as he hollered, "Sergeant Mulkowski, get your ass out here!"

A bewildered master sergeant appeared at the door. "Yes sir, can I help you?"

"You're damn right you can. Get every enlisted man down here on the double by the main path."

Without hesitation, Mike started through the row of tents. "Okay, everybody out. On the double. Line up on the assembly path—now!"

A sudden outpouring of GIs in various stages of disarray, including several clad only in their shorts, rushed down from their living quarters and quickly lined up in formation.

"Attention!" the sergeant barked. "Captain Lewis would like to talk with you."

His lips still quivering with rage, the officer strode in front of the hastily assembled group of men.

"Alright," he demanded. "Who was the crazy son of a bitch that shot the Chinese peasant down on the field a half an hour ago?"

Blank stares provided the only answer he got. Nobody said a word. The rain really started to come down. The men were getting soaked. George had forgotten to get his raincoat. The private was standing at the side of the aligned men, secretly hoping somebody would confess his guilt so they all could get the hell out of there. The captain was pacing back and forth in front of the group trying to detect some clue as to the responsible party.

"Okay, if nobody wants to admit it, you will all stay out here at attention until I find out."

He motioned to Mike. "That is an order, Sergeant!"

"Yes sir," replied the grim-faced non-com, his fatigues thoroughly drenched.

As the captain turned to leave, a weak voice managed to make itself heard. "I did the shooting, sir."

Lewis wheeled about and retraced his steps till he stopped in front of a shaking, pale-faced airman with the stripes of a corporal on his sleeve.

The officer stared angrily at the frightened man. "Are you the one that shot the Chinese peasant down on the field?"

"Yes sir," was the meek answer.

The captain continued, "Do you realize what the results of your damn foolishness could be?"

"Yes sir."

"Do you realize you have jeopardized the trust we have been trying to build up with the local people?"

"Yes sir."

"Do you know you will probably face a general court martial and spend maybe the next twenty years of your life in prison?"

"Yes sir." The man began sobbing uncontrollably.

Finally, his rage having softened somewhat, the captain turned to Mulkowski. "Sergeant, this man is to be restricted to the base and transferred, under guard, to Chungking, where he will stand trial. You may dismiss your men."

Goerig watched his superior officer as he left the group of rain-soaked men, who were slowly walking back to their tents.

The captain's face was still tense as he looked back at the unfortunate boy being led away by a husky non-com.

He murmured, "Dammit, why do things like this have to happen?"

The captain and the private sat around the warm glow of a charcoal fire in George's room. Their wet clothes were dripping from hangers tied to the ceiling beam. Warm leather flying jackets draped over their shoulders slowly created a comfortable feeling. Goerig glanced over at his superior.

"You know, sir, I think you were a little hasty in your decision about that man. A general court martial in wartime is a real serious offense."

"What the hell else should I have done?"

Goerig tried to reason. "But you never gave him a chance to try and explain his side of the story. He most likely was shooting at that damn mongrel dog and hit the peasant by mistake. That is no court martial offense."

The captain glared at his aide. "He still shot him, didn't he? He admitted it. What's the difference?"

Slowly the private got up. He drained the glass in his hand. "I'll tell you what the difference is. Now you just set your glass aside and listen to me for a few minutes."

George was beginning to warm up to the discussion he knew would a difficult one. Sitting back down, however, the emotional tension that had been building up inside of him seemed to temporarily abate somewhat.

"Captain," Goerig began, "several months ago a certain person tried to have me court martialed. If he had succeeded, he would have destroyed my future. To him, I was a mere inanimate object that had crossed his path and was to be eliminated. Fortunately, I was saved by a friend who figured I had received a bum deal. It was then that I got transferred to China, thanks to General Chenault."

Lewis remained silent as his head was bowed and he gazed at the burning embers in the fireplace.

George continued, "The incident today was an accident. I went back to the campsite and talked to the corporal and to Mike. According to them, the man was shooting at that dog on the field and thought it was fair game. He did not intend to harm anyone. I believe him, and I think that is the way that most of the men feel."

Receiving no response, the private went over to his bed and turned back the covers.

"Please give it some consideration, sir. A certain person gave me a break once, and I hope you can do the same. Good night."

The dying, flickering flames outlined the drawn features of a face engrossed in deep thought.

The following day, word that Corporal Mullally had been released from restriction and restored to his former rank had a tremendous impact on the close-knit "recon" group.

The previous night, Captain Ho and Lieutenant Lee had met with Captain Lewis in the evening following the very strenuous day on which the unfortunate event had occurred. The Chinese engineer had opened the conversation.

"Captain Lewis, a few months ago Mister George prevailed upon us to save the life of a worthless soldier who had committed an unforgivable crime and should have been shot." He paused and then continued. "Today, we would like to discuss the fate of one of your airmen who accidently shot a Chinese peasant and has to face . . . what do you call it?" Lee hesitated as he tried to recall the proper words.

George interrupted. "A court martial, sir." Then he added, "It is a very serious offense, especially during time of war. If convicted, he would be dishonorably discharged and sent to prison."

Lee looked at Captain Lewis pleadingly. "We would like to have this man freed of all charges."

The ensuing silence lasted for over a minute as no further discussion seemed necessary.

Sergeant Mulkowski, who had accompanied the Chinese officers, eagerly rushed forward and grasped the captain's hand. "Thank you, sir. He is a good man. You will not regret this action, sir."

Lewis returned the handshake and promptly announced, "Now, why the hell don't you all get out of here so we can take care of some important business?"

As they left, the door was closed behind them. The captain looked at his aide. "You know, I would have made a lousy prosecuting attorney."

"Don't worry about it, sir. I was behind you all the way and, after all, I had one year in law school."

"You were a big help." Lewis sarcastically laughed. "Come on, let's get down to that business I told those guys about."

He walked over to his duffel bag and drew out a bottle of Scotch. "Cocktails before dinner?" he asked. "This represents our business for the night."

Goerig quickly stood up and raised his hand in protest. "Oh no, it doesn't. We definitely have some unfinished business to discuss."

"What's that?"

"The little matter of promotion before this war is ended, plus a litle bonus. We've talked this matter before."

The captain poured two stiff drinks and grinned. "I've already recommended you for your old sergeant stripes, but it takes time. Now what the hell is this bonus deal you are talking about? You are in the Army, not in civilian life."

George persisted. "Okay, okay, how many men in this man's Army have the responsibility I have here? Also, look at the results we've been getting. I should have something encouraging to write home to my wife about."

"What do you suggest?" Lewis asked, smiling.

"How about the Bronze Star Medal?" came the quick reply.

Lewis hesitated, then said, "Well, you can't get it without a recommendation. So I'd suggest you get your ass over to that table and start writing."

"What do I say?"

"What did you just get through saying to me?"

"Gotcha. Mind if I have a drink first?"

"As long as it is business, be my guest."

Within the next several hours, the two men had finished the bottle of Scotch and eaten a large meal. They were sitting at the table discussing the events of the day and listening to their favorite records by Tokyo Rose when the captain stood up.

"Got anything to drink? I'm getting thirsty as hell."

"Sure," George replied. "A couple of cans of grapefruit juice. If you are thinking about any more alcoholic beverages, you are out of luck. You know we just killed off that bottle of Scotch before supper."

Lewis glanced briefly up at the shelf by the window sill.

"What are those bottles of puda ju up there for? Decorations?"

Goerig then remembered the partially filled bottles of rice wine he had failed to finish. Over a period of time, he had managed to accumulate about a half a dozen of them. The porous onion corks had not prevented a horde of tiny gnats to be lured to their doom by the attraction of the sweet smelling, potent liquid. A thin layer of the black, very dead insects covered the top of the remaining puda ju. George had merely forgotten to throw the bottles out. Suddenly, he realized what was on the officer's mind.

"Oh no, you're not thinking what I think you are thinking, are you?" he asked incredulously.

"Why not?" Lewis answered. "I've done it before when we ran out of American booze. I'm still healthy with no side effects I know of. Come on, get a couple of glasses. I'll show you that a little added foreign fermentation doesn't hurt anyone."

Producing a new, clean handkerchief from his pocket, the captain walked over to the shelf and brought down one of the bottles. It was almost half full with a quarter of an inch of floating insects sloshing about inside. He spread the cloth over the glass, making a slight funnel shape indentation into the top by pushing down his finger in the middle of the glass.

"Okay, start pouring," he ordered.

The private hesitated and then shrugged his shoulders. "If you say so, sir. I'll try anything once."

Following several minutes of the macabre operation, the two found themselves with three full glasses of the pure potent liquid at their disposal. George expertly mixed two drinks, with an ample addition of grapefruit juice, and raised his glass, offering a questionable toast.

"Well, here's to you, captain. Cheers."

With a satisfied grin on his face, the officer jokingly replied, "Swebien."

After having several more of the stimulating beverages, the two were convinced they had discovered the ingredients of a terrific new cocktail, which actually at the time was the standard drink among the GIs in China.

The loquacity of their conversation related back through many phases of their lives during previous years. Finally, the captain's face began getting red and flushed. The slurriness of his speech indicated to Goerig that it was time for both of them to go to bed. Lewis complacently agreed and stumbled over to his cot. He was soon sound asleep. George sat back and reflected on the evening's happenings. He silently marveled in his drunken stupor at his superior's ingenuity of turning a dry time into a wet one. It showed the true value of the man.

If only his wife Helen could have been there to share their unique cocktails. Well, you can't have everything.

The following morning was bright and clear; George woke the captain to remind him that they had been invited to be dinner guests at the home of a wealthy Chinese merchant in a neighboring town. Captain Ho and Lee, along with several other prominent citizens, were to join them. Goerig was wondering what mode of travel they were to take as the accommodation of the two jeeps was hardly large enough for the entire group.

Shortly before noon, a happy group of men and women gathered outside the compound. The cloudless blue sky indicated a very pleasant day for the trip.

Suddenly, the captain nudged Goerig on the arm. "Those can't be for us, are they?"

The private looked around and noticed a Chinese boy leading two saddled horses up the road towards them. They were pony size, and small ponies at that.

George quipped, "Looks like we have a couple of midget entries for the Kentucky Derby. What kind of a jockey are you, or do they have horses in New York?"

Lewis laughed. "If you don't mind, I'II take the big one."

George countered. "Alright, I'll take the small one. But don't blame me if I wear out my boots dragging on the ground."

With all the Chinese walking, Goerig felt embarrassed astride his docile mount. However, Lee explained that the horses had been sent over by their host for the day and were reserved only for the American guests. While he had small misgivings about riding, George knew his companions would be in far better shape after the trip was over.

As they bravely set forth, memories of the adventures of Don Quixote crossed the private's mind. Fortunately, there was not a windmill in sight to be challenged.

The day was a complete success. There were approximately eighty to a hundred guests at the dinner served outside on a patio adjacent to the impressive residence that seemed out of place in the rural area. The host was a very exuberant and genial person whose lack of knowledge of the English language proved no barrier to an enjoyable day.

Goerig was pleasantly surprised when his captain repeatedly passed up the innumerable *"gombey"* toasts in lieu of the more conservative *"swebiens."* George believed his superior must have had the long journey home in mind even if the day still had a way to go.

By the time it came to say goodbye to their smiling host, however, neither of the Americans was feeling any pain. They politely refused to ride the ponies back to Laifeng, stating the walk would be better for them. And it definitely was.

It was a tired but happy group of people who said goodbye at the gates of the compound. Lieutenant Lee had been indispensable as their interpreter, translating Chinese into English and visa-versa. By this time, Captain Ho had been learning the meaning of the basic words of the English language and was beginning to be able to carry on a conversation. Despite the wonderful happenings during the day, the evening was due to end tragically.

As the captain and private were preparing for bed, a very excited but solemn-faced Lieutenant Lee entered Goerig's room. The Chinese hesitated as he groped for words and then finally sadly announced, "I am very sorry to tell you this. We just heard over the radio that your President Roosevelt died today. Captain Ho and I give you our deepest sympathies."

The two Americans sat down and blankly stared at each other. The sudden impact of such tragic and saddening news slowly began to have its effect upon the two men. It seemed like a member of their own family had passed away. The great man had been the bulwark of the nation in its fight against the Axis countries. He had united the people in their valiant effort to destroy the enemy. It was not till later when the actual, stunning truth and the extent of the seriousness of his continuing illness and constant pain would be revealed to the public. He was truly a great and unforgettable man.

Harry S. Truman was now the new president. He would be undertaking a tremendous challenge. Would the former haberdasher from Independence, Missouri, be capable of handling the vast problems he had to face? Time would tell. At least he had a great and willing nation united behind him.

CHAPTER TWENTY

Goerig was standing by the portal of the compound talking to Lieutenant Lee when Lewis drove up in his battered jeep. The captain had just come down from the radio station. When he jumped out of the jeep he was grinning as he walked over to the two men.

"Well, it looks like it won't be long now. Just got the news that some kind of an atom bomb was dropped on Hiroshima. I guess it damn near blew the entire city off the map. The Japs are going crazy. They say it had the equivalent of twenty thousand tons of TNT. That's quite a blast. Come on, we'll go back up to the station and see what other news there is."

Amid a cloud of dust the three men headed back over to the radio shack. The date was August sixth, nineteen hundred and forty-five. It was to be the most memorable date in the history of warfare. They didn't realize it then but the world was just entering into a new era. The Atomic Age had officially begun.

After another of the devastating bombs had been dropped on Nagasaki a few days later, it just seemed to be a matter of time until the final collapse of the Japanese Empire was a certainty.

On August 15th, Japan agreed to unconditional surrender. The war was over. It was time to go home. But the Fourteenth had other ideas for Private Goerig.

"Well, your orders just came through, boy. Want to know where you are going from here?" Captain Lewis tauntingly waved a sheet of paper in front of George's face.

"Yeah, if it's not too much trouble," Goerig answered. "Couldn't be stateside, could it?"

He looked at his aide with feigned sadness. "Not so lucky. You are to report to headquarters. They are sending you to Sian."

"Sian!" Goerig bellowed. "Why hell, that's the first place the Reds will take over when they start to tangle with Chiang Kai-shek. That's no place for me!"

The Captain hesitated a moment, seeming to relish the frustrated look on the private's face. He winked at Lieutenant Lee and continued.

"I figured you wouldn't care for that place, so I decided to change your orders."

George stared at his superior in amazement. "But, you can't just change those orders. What would the colonel say? It's a helluva a time for you to get into any trouble. Let it go. I'll take my chances on Sian."

Lewis took another paper out of his pocket and gave it to Goerig. As the latter began to read it, the captain interrupted.

"I just finished writing that one up. It's your new orders. You are to catch the first transport to Shanghai."

He waved the remaining document in his hand. "I'm the one who is going Stateside. By the time they start looking for you, I'll be a civilian in New York. As long as you hold on to that paper, you are in the clear. But for your own sake, don't lose it."

Goerig's mouth fell open. "Why you wonderful, sweet old bastard. I could kiss you for that."

"Save it for the gals in Shanghai. Whether you know it or not, Shanghai used to be known as the 'Paris of the East.' In some ways, I wish I was going with you, but I'll take New York. Now or anytime."

Lewis looked up at the clear blue sky with its fragments of fluffy white clouds casually drifting by. "Should be a transport stopping by tomorrow if the weather is okay. There will be a load of Chinese troops aboard. The pilot has been instructed to stop by and pick you up. You had better be ready when he gets here."

George excused himself as he realized he had one important chore to do. He went in search of Lieutenant Lee.

Goerig had been approached by the Chinese engineer on behalf of the contractors. Since the war was over, the contractors were uncertain as to the situation that had created. Future work had been canceled, but the contractors had been paid in advance. What was going to happen next? The Chinese contractors thought that perhaps taking a friendly approach to Mister George might be appropriate. How right they were.

Captain Lewis had taken a short trip over to the residence of the merchant who had given the dinner party for them just shortly before. He had been notified that some pieces of jade the man had promised him were available. It was a small token of appreciation for the dedicated officer who had done so much for the Chinese cause.

In the meantime, Goerig came prepared for his own little meeting with his Chinese contractors. Lieutenant Lee was presiding. The private wasted no time and quickly came to the point.

"Alright, Lieutenant, I'd like to clarify my position in regard to my last trip to Chungking. At that time these people"—he indicated the four representatives sitting around the table—"said that they would provide me with money so I could purchase various gifts to take back home with me. Unfortunately, I had to leave in a hurry so I was unable to take them up on their gratuitous offer. However, I have been notified that I am to go to Shanghai tomorrow. I would also like to do some shopping in that city. I have three cartons of cigarettes here. In exchange for them, I would like to give you the equivalent of three thousand American dollars in Chinese currency."

Lee patiently interpreted George's brief but pointed talk. A hurried consultation took place among the agents. After a few quick nods of heads, they turned their smiling, agreeable faces to the lieutenant.

George's good friend and helpful benefactor, in turn, took Goerig aside and assured him, "You will have your money by noon, today. It will be delivered to your room."

Goerig smilingly thanked the engineer and handed over the three cartons of cigarettes. He then silently thought to himself. "George, you damn fool, you could have gotten ten thousand just as easy, maybe more. But why be greedy? After all, you are only a private."

The inflationary boom had created an increase in the quantity of paper money needed for even small sums. Goerig was in the process of deciding what articles of clothing he would have to discard in order to accommodate his newfound treasure. There was a knock at the door. As the private opened it, Chen entered with a gunny sack in his skinny arms. He proceeded over to the bed and joyfully dumped the contents of the bag. It consisted of lovely fresh packages of green currency.

"Ding hao, ding hao!" he shouted.

"You can say that again, Chen. This is one little bundle those thieving bastards won't be taking back to Chungking with them. I'm sure I can put it to better use in Shanghai. Come on, help me stash this loot in my bag and make it solid. I want some room for my clothes. But, hell, I can always get more khakis from the Air Force when they get to Shanghai."

The houseboy immediately got the message, as George used his hands to indicate what he wanted. The boy was rapidly becoming adept in Chinese sign language, which was another minor achievement in the life of Private Goerig. Finally, his pressed clothes were deposited on top of the money and the bag was safely stowed under his bed.

As he straightened up, George remembered there was one more thing he had to do. It concerned his former houseboy.

"Where is Chang?" he inquired of Chen.

The boy's eyes widened and he shook his head to indicate he was having no more to do with his former friend.

"Come on, we'll see Lieutenant Lee, I want to wish the kid goodbye, even if he did screw up a bit."

They walked out the door over to the engineer's office. Lee was bent over his drafting table and intently absorbed in drawing some lines on a sheet of plans. Upon hearing the two enter the room, he looked up and smiled broadly.

"Mister George, what a pleasant surprise. What can I do for you?"

"Lieutenant, I have come to ask a favor of you."

"Anything, anything," he answered.

"I want to see my former houseboy, Chang, and wish him goodbye."

Lee's smile vanished and a frown came over his face. He hesitated a moment and then stated, "Chang is being punished and he is not to talk with anybody, not even his own comrades. They have been ordered to ignore him completely. However, since you request to see him, you certainly may."

Turning to Chen, he ordered, "Take Mister George over to where Chang is working."

"Thank you, Lieutenant, very much, I appreciate this. I hope to see you and Captain Ho before I leave and wish you both a fond goodbye. However, I will take this opportunity to thank you for what you have done for me, and I have certainly enjoyed my stay here."

Lee nodded his head in acknowledgement as George warmly clasped his hand. Chen started for the door. They found Chang working with several other soldiers, using rakes and shovels to clean up an area outside the compound. A small pile of brush was briskly burning to one side while additional twigs and debris were being tossed on it.

As they approached the former houseboy, he looked up apprehensively; Chen moved forward and quickly relieved him of any fears he might have had. George put out his hand in a friendly gesture. The lad hesitated and then warmly grasped it. The small amount of English he had been able to learn came to his stuttering lips.

"Tha, tha, thank you, Mister George." Uncontrolled tears rolled down his cheeks.

The sudden, startled expressions of his fellow workers quickly changed to looks of amazement as they gathered around Chang. With that simple gesture, Goerig figured that the boy had maybe at least regained a portion of the "face" he had temporarily lost. It seemed he had been accepted back in the group, which was now chattering happily. George turned and hurriedly left as tears began to roll down his cheeks. It was several minutes before he was able to regain his composure.

The morning before George was to leave, Captain Lewis drove up with the two sergeants who were to replace the private. He hollered to George as the private was leaving the compound. "Come on, boy, there are a few things I want to go over with you on finalizing out this job, before you leave. Hop in!"

Goerig climbed in next to the captain, and with a screaming of the tires, they spun around and headed down the hill.

"Okay, back there, you guys start taking notes on what Goerig has to say, and be sure you get it right. Between the two of you, you should be able to get it straight."

Both men had a notebook and a pencil in their hands as they tried desperately to hold on to the side of the jeep as the captain bounced along.

"Sir, how the hell are they going to be able to write with the way you're driving?" George yelled.

Lewis quickly straightened up from his bent position over the wheel and slowed the vehicle down. Sarcastically, he turned to Goerig. "Yes sir, I'll drive more carefully."

Since the future work was going to be discontinued in lieu of the fact that the Fourteenth had no more use for the airfield, it was to be left in a suitable condition. The four men drove past the unfinished project as several hundred laboring coolies were cleaning up the existing runway for the final phasing out of all construction work. Goerig pointed out where mounds of unused rock could be dispersed and locations where the extra crushed rock surfacing could he most beneficially spread. That would take care of the obstacles alongside of the runway that might prove disastrous to a wayward plane.

They continued to the far end of the airstrip as the private showed the captain where partially excavated ditches should be completed to provide proper drainage for the surface water that accumulated after occasional rainstorms.

As Lewis swung the jeep around to head back to the compound, Goerig asked, "Is there anything else, sir, I can help you with before I leave?"

The answer came quick. "You know damn well. We have some more unfinished business to go over in your room." Looking back at the two subdued sergeants in the rear, he finished, "After we drop these boys off."

A few hours later, while George stood at the edge of the unfinished new runway impatiently waiting for his overdue transport, he hastily reflected back over his interesting and enjoyable stay among the hospitable and friendly people of the small town of Laifeng. The sincere feelings and simple pleasures of the local inhabitants had made a lasting and invaluable impression on the American private.

As he glanced back emotionally at the rolling hills and innumerable rice paddies that made up the rural landscape, he had learned to enjoy so much. Goerig sadly shook his head. It had all been so wonderful. Now that the war was finally over, what would Shanghai and the future hold for him? What would be the final outcome?

His nostalgic reverie and thoughts of the days ahead were abruptly interrupted by the familiar drone of his long-awaited C-47. Captain Lewis, who had been talking with Lieutenant Lee, walked over and warmly put his arm around his aide's shoulder.

"George, I can't start to tell you how much you have meant to me down here. It's been a pleasure working with you, and I'll never forget the wonderful times we have had together."

Unexpected tears began to slowly dim the private's eyes as he turned and finally began to realize this would probably be the last time he would see his lovable and generous superior.

Grasping the officer's hand, George fervently managed to express his heartfelt feelings. "Sir, I can't thank you enough for what you have done.

I'll always remember my stay in Laifeng. Someday, maybe, I'll be able to get back to New York and look you up."

The captain eased the parting tension with a hearty laugh. "Be sure and do that. We'll have a ball."

Goerig didn't look back as he walked over to the waiting transport.

CHAPTER TWENTY-ONE

Walking through the door of the C-47 transport that was to carry him to Shanghai, Private Goerig immediately became aware of approximately twenty grinning and laughing Chinese soldiers dressed in clean, pressed uniforms of the Nationalist Army who were occupying most of the bucket seats.

"Ding hao, ding hao!" were the words that greeted George as he moved forward to an empty place next to the pilot's compartment. The private looked back at his fellow passengers and somberly wondered to himself, "Is the Generalissimo going to try and convince the people of Shanghai that these men actually won the war against the Japanese?"

Goerig then reflected back to the conversations he had had with his friends in Liangshan and Enshih. "Yes, Chiang Kai-shek is a very crafty person. He will use the United States as long as his personal ambitions are achieved. He will then resort to his egotistical role as the victorious savior of the war weary people of China." How true, these prophetic words were now becoming a reality.

George had fallen asleep to the steady drone of the plane's engines when the sudden blast of a cold breeze startled him and he immediately became wide awake. He looked around to locate its source. The transport doors had been flung open and, unbelievingly, he watched as several of the Chinese soldiers were throwing two of their airsick comrades out of the plane. The private was dumbfounded.

Without thinking of the possible consequences, George hammered on the pilot's door and quickly rushed back to the rear of the plane, stumbling over the outstretched legs of the complacent passengers. Not realizing what could have happened to him, Goerig smashed his fist into the face of the closest self-appointed assassin. Reaching for the other startled soldier, he roughly threw him back to the rear of the fuselage.

At this time, a husky co-pilot appeared at Goerig's side. Between the two of them, they managed to close the swinging door. The private then returned to his seat, opened his barracks bag, and removed a holstered forty-five. Turning back to the gaping faces of the suddenly cowed soldiers, he calmly announced, "Now, you rotten bastards, the first man that leaves his seat is going to be shot."

Despite the fact that the men had no understanding of the English language, it was very apparent that they got the message. The co-pilot, standing next to George, reassured him, "Buddy, if you need any more help, just rap on the door."

"Thanks, but I don't think I will have any more trouble."

The co-pilot disappeared back into his compartment as Goerig took his seat again. The balance of the trip was uneventful. By the time they landed at the Shanghai airport, George reasoned that some of the nicely creased pants of Chiang's victorious troops were going to be badly soiled.

As the twin engine transport gracefully circled the vast metropolis of Shanghai, a city of four million people, George excitedly looked down at his future temporary home. "My God," he jokingly murmured, to himself, "Laifeng was never like this. What next?"

It was then that a fearful apprehension began to come over the private. Despite the war being over, he anxiously wondered what kind of a reception he would receive from the occupying Japanese troops, who still were in charge of most of the activities in and around the fabled city.

He had managed to have a brief conversation with his friend, the co-pilot, regarding the situation existing at the airport. All in all, it had seemed rather confusing. The lieutenant had made one trip transporting the Chinese troops a few days previously. The flight crew had been looking forward to visiting Shanghai for a few hours at least. They had been told in no uncertain terms that the former capital of China was "off limits" to all United States military personnel. George was not wrong in assuming it was on direct orders from Generalissimo Chiang Kai-shek. After all, it was the Chinese who won the war, wasn't it? At least that is what the latter wanted the people of Shanghai to believe.

However, there was one American private who was convinced that one way or another, he was going find a way to get into the former "Paris of the East." He did not anticipate coming in as a conquering hero, only as a curious GI-tourist.

The perfect landing at their final destination relieved the private of the tension he had been carrying throughout the trip. Tossing the unused gun back in his barracks bag, he waited for the Chinese to leave the plane. Finally, he got up, heaved a sigh of relief, and headed for the open door. As he walked towards the air base's terminal, George was met by two courteous Japanese soldiers.

He knew the war was over, but he didn't realize that everything had not been finalized regarding the transition from the defeated Japanese, who were still in control, over to the Chinese government. Meanwhile the departing Nationalist troops were eagerly surrounding the pair of Nip soldiers who had just welcomed the American private.

"Ding hao! Ding hao!" they were shouting as they stupidly fawned over their former enemy.

Goerig couldn't believe his eyes. He watched as the two Japanese insolently turned their backs on the so-called conquerors. The private fervently wished Chiang Kai-shek could have been present to witness the arrival of his triumphant elite troops.

Quietly enjoying the bizarre situation, he wandered slowly through the terminal building the Japanese had used as a final headquarters. Rifles, carbines, revolvers, and other tools of war had been neatly piled on separate tables. Enviously, he thought to himself, "What a wonderful place for a souvenir hunter."

Still apprehensive about his temporary hosts, he decided to get out of the building and find a ride into Shanghai. As if in response to his wishes, he watched a battered Japanese army truck approaching. Goerig impatiently waved his hand. The vehicle stopped and he eagerly climbed in.

"Shanghai! Shanghai!" he yelled and gestured with his arm toward the general locality of the city as he'd seen it before landing. The Japanese driver looked at the brash American with a startled and perplexed expression on his face. Finally, after the private was convinced they were headed in the right direction, he settled back on the hard, canvas seat. Occasionally glancing at his involuntary chauffer, George found himself in a very relaxed and exhilarated mood. He actually felt like saying, "Home, James." However, he was reasonably certain the driver's name was not James.

On the busy road to the fabled city, the traffic was dominated primarily by Japanese military vehicles, although there was one convoy of United States Army trucks loaded with Chinese soldiers and led by an impatient Chinese officer driving a jeep. The excited man was constantly sounding his horn at the slow-moving vehicle in which Goerig was riding. Finally, the unimpressed private motioned for his driver to pull over to the side of the road and let the convoy pass.

As the trucks went by with their open beds overloaded with exuberant Chinese troops, George thought to himself, "Oh boy, here comes Chiang's advance publicity team to conduct their own victory parade." Suddenly, his attitude changed to one of bitter recollection. The absence of two very notable personalities who had played such an important part in the victory melodrama that had help save the Nationalist Government was being made very conspicuous by their uninvited presence. However, they had one unauthorized private silently rooting for them. Their unforgettable names were General Joseph Stillwell and General Clare Chenault.

Eventually, George's Japanese driver was able to wend his way through the crowded streets of Shanghai amidst the abundance of rickshaws and bicycle traffic. The private was on the alert for one tall building that dominated the others by its height. It was the Parke Hotel. He had previously noted it in several pictures of the downtown section of the famous city. He had also read where it was definitely the finest of all the hotels in that locale.

Suddenly Goerig recognized what he thought was his final objective. Hollering for the still-dazed driver to pull over to the curb, he patiently waited for him to stop. Jumping out, the private hurriedly grabbed his barracks bag and turned around. "Thanks, buddy. I'll do something for you sometime."

The dumbfounded Japanese simply shook his head with the same confused expression he had worn during the entire trip.

Goerig expectantly walked over to the imposing edifice he had decided was going to be his temporary home. Slowly, he became aware of various groups of happy, hilarious people, primarily English, who were laughing, weeping, and throwing their arms around each other. It then occurred to him that he should try and get in on the action.

He quickly appraised the unexpected, exuberant reunion of the recently released internees. Two very attractive young females immediately became the object of his attention. One was a tall, shapely blond and the other was a short, pert-looking brunette. George casually approached the two, doffed his service cap, and smilingly introduced himself.

"I am an American and a stranger in this town. I wonder if you could direct me to the Parke Hotel?"

Their widened eyes expressed the girls' amusement as they looked at each other incredulously. "A Yankee soldier!" the blonde excitedly yelled. "Where did you come from?"

"Oh, from over there," George calmly replied as he vaguely pointed in a westerly direction. "How about you two?"

The short one quickly answered, "We have just been released from an internment camp. We have spent the entire war here outside Shanghai." She hesitated, "But what are we talking for? Here is something special for you, Yank."

Eagerly, the unabashed girl threw her arms around George's neck and pulling him close to her ample bosom and began to cover his lips with her moist and tender mouth. Barely managing to maintain his balance, the private dropped his barracks bag to the pavement. Finally, the brunette reluctantly stepped back and as Goerig was trying to catch his breath, she murmured softly, "That was for starters, Yank. When am I going to see you again?"

A pleading, plaintive voice behind her interrupted and anxiously asked, "How about me? I haven't kissed a handsome man like him for years."

The tall blonde doll had her hair neatly combed back from a saucy, sexy face with pouting lips. "At least, don't I get one kiss?"

Her rounded breasts were tantalizingly trying to push out of the top of her white blouse, and the slightly hidden deep cleavage gave her a certain magnetic charm. George purposely walked over and gently raised a dimpled chin. A puckered mouth lifted towards his lips. He could feel the girl passionately respond as she quickly rose on the tip of her toes and tried to mash a certain part of her anatomy into Goerig's. As she succeeded, he also rose to the occasion and obligingly pulled her closer.

The girl then proceeded to agonizingly tease the private with the tip of her tongue until the latter forcibly culminated the anticipated kiss. They stood closely entwined for a long moment when, finally, she breathlessly released him and leaned back. Gasping, she warmly asked, "How was that for openers, Yank?"

George quickly replied, "You are great, baby."

It was then that he embarrassingly noticed that a group, all laughing, had silently surrounded the three and began enthusiastically clapping. Grabbing both girls by their arms, the private headed for the welcoming doors of the Parke Hotel. Before entering, however, he turned and bowed to his appreciative audience. He then whispered to newfound friends, "Let's leave the encore for later."

They both agreed, laughed, and eagerly joined George, the three of them nonchalantly strolling towards the main desk in the lobby. A tall, affable faced Englishman, with an assured, suave manner, stood impassively at attention.

"What may I do for you, sir?" he haughtily asked.

The private confidently answered, "I would like the best suite of rooms you have available. Preferably with one large single bed for three. My name is George Goerig. I am a member of United States Air Force and I will be staying here temporarily until my superiors arrive. I will pay for the accommodations myself and any room services I might request."

Goerig looked down for his barracks bag, which he thought he had brought in with him. Incredulously, he gasped, "Oh my God, where is it?" He rushed for the entrance of the lobby but abruptly stopped when he saw two elderly gentlemen walking toward him carrying the missing bag between them. One of the gray-haired men smiled and said, "Hi, old chap, did you forget something?"

George's relieved expression was apparent. "Oh, did I ever, you'll never know. Thanks a million." He silently thought to himself, "Well, not quite a million, but enough, I hope." He profusely thanked both gentlemen again and walked back to the waiting clerk at the desk.

After producing a registration card for the private to sign, he graciously announced, "Glad to have you aboard, sir, and my regards to your fellow comrades who did such a splendid job on the 'Krauts and the Nips.

As George wrote his name on the extended card, he glanced up and asked, "You must have been in the Navy, right? What with your welcome aboard?"

"Oh no, sir. I was a desk clerk right here when the war started. I was interned with the rest of my friends, along with some Navy fellows. I could not help but pick up some of their jargon." He hesitated. "I also hope that I can forget a certain portion of their version of the English language before I go back to London." Laughing, he continued, "I really don't believe my mother would approve, you know."

Lightly tapping the desk call bell, he beckoned to a dapper young man in a page boy's uniform.

"Johnnie, take Mister Goerig's suitcase. He hesitated as he looked down and corrected himself. "Rather, his belongings up to suite 601." Turning back to the impatient threesome, he proudly remarked, "Believe me, this is the best suite in the hotel. I'm sure you will enjoy it. If you want anything, just call for room service. Please have a good evening." He looked enviously at the private as the latter escorted his lovely companions to the elevators.

George glanced back over his shoulder and said, "I'm sure we will, you old sailor, you."

The clerk smiled.

The three followed the bell boy out of the elevator across the hall and into a spacious room.

"Blimey!" shouted the blonde. "It's like the Grand Central Station."

George casually replied, "Come on, gals, there is nothing too good for you." He pointed to a closet. "Hang your coats over there."

The bellboy raised a window, and as he started to go asked hesitantly, "Is there anything you might like, sir?"

The reply was quick. "You damn right there is. How about it, girls? Scotch?"

The two quickly nodded their heads as George took out several Chinese bank notes. He handed them to Johnnie and ordered, "Scotch, the best in the house, with bottles of soda and a lot of ice." As the boy headed for the door, he added, "Bring up a menu also."

Meanwhile the English girls were "oh-ing" and "ah-ing" over the king-size bed and the pink, silken sheets.

"Blimey, they are so beautiful and so soft," the blonde dreamily remarked.

George politely interrupted their reverie as he walked over and apologetically introduced himself. "I'm very sorry, I should have introduced myself before. My name is George Goerig of the Fourteenth Air Force. I don't believe I've had the honor of your acquaintance." He laughed. "May I have your names so I don't get you two confused?"

The tall blonde smiled pleasantly. "I am Faye," and nodding her head toward her dark-haired friend, added, "This is Laverne."

"Well, that was easy, wasn't it?" the private laughed. "When was the last time you slept in a bed like that one, if I'm not being too personal?"

Unintentionally, it seemed as though the private had pressed a magic button. The two girls simultaneously threw themselves on the soft, yielding mattress and began bouncing up and down on their packs. Their skirts naturally obeyed the law of gravity as they slid down around their enticing hips, exposing a pair of pink, lace panties that were conveniently covering a precious part of their anatomy.

"It seems like centuries!" Laverne cried in ecstasy. "I could stay here all night and love every minute of it."

"Me too," echoed Faye as they continued to enjoy their newfound relaxing comfort.

Goerig, not wishing to miss any of the fun, made a short dive over to the foot of the bed and happily landed safely between the two of them.

"I hope I get the message loud and clear!" he exclaimed.

In amorous response he soon found himself engulfed amidst two pair of arms and entwined legs. Laverne started nibbling on one ear while Faye pulled at the knot on his tie. Hastily throwing the cravat on the floor, she began to unbutton his shirt. Then, unexpectedly, George sat up. He had stupidly remembered the Scotch and soda order that had not come.

"What about our drinks before we get started?" he plaintively asked. "Personally, I'm thirsty as hell."

"Oh that can wait," Laverne impatiently whispered.

"Hold on a minute. I've got to make a call."

Rolling over the bewildered Faye, George landed on the floor and picked up the phone. "Where the hell is our booze?" he hollered.

Then, apologetically, he lowered his voice. "Get Johnnie on the phone."

After a minute or two a subdued voice answered, "Yes sir, what can I do for you, Mister Goerig?"

"Johnnie, is it possible for you to pick up two negligees from any of the stores off the lobby when you bring up the Scotch?"

"Mine's an eight!" yelled Laverne.

"Make mine a twelve!" echoed Faye.

The bellboy heard the voices as he replied, "Yes sir, Righto. Will be up as soon as I can."

"Hurry it up," the private pleaded as his rising emotions were starting to get the better of him. Then he glanced over at the bed. It was empty.

Running water could be heard coming from the bathroom. An urgent, teasing voice beckoned from the darkened shower stall. "Come on and join in on the fun. It's big enough."

Goerig needed no further invitation. He kicked off his shoes and slipped down his pants. One remaining button on his shirt was torn off as he hurriedly doffed the rest of his clothes.

Inadvertently, George stumbled over an ottoman as he clumsily dashed toward the sound of the running water. Eagerly, he pulled back the shower curtain. The stall was empty. Sounds of muffled giggles came from the adjacent bathroom. Goerig ducked back from the cascading water and reached for the nearby light switch.

Standing completely nude with the exception of a bath towel loosely wrapped around them were his uninhibited bedmates. Faye was the first to remove her scanty clothing, proudly revealing a firm pair of full, rounded breasts with budding, pink nipples. Her slender waist tapered down to the flawless curved hips with the triangular patch of hair indicating she was truly a blonde.

Not to be outdone, her companion hesitantly uncovered her petite but luxurious body, disclosing her own tempting orbs for the private's approval. His reaction was immediate as he walked over to the smaller girl and started to put his arms around her enticing figure and bend down to kiss the inviting lips. The girl surprisingly stepped back a pace and gently placed a dainty finger over George's mouth.

"Not now. Come on, it's shower time and we are getting cold. The evening is young and we will attend to that later."

Goerig's disappointment at the negative reaction was apparent, to say the least. However, the resignedly shrugged his shoulders and started to mentally lay future plans for the balance of the night. She was right, he still had plenty of time.

The three pushed their way through the narrow entrance and were soon enjoying the warm spray of the cascading water. Both girls quickly reached for the bars of soap on the wall frame and began giving their temporarily frustrated host a warm, vigorous lathering. Laverne, being the shortest, was standing in front of George doing a thorough job rubbing his tense body. Meanwhile, he in turn was gently fondling two firm breasts being intentionally offered for their mutual pleasure.

Teasingly, he lightly brushed the rising tips of her breasts with his fingers. Finally, be slipped his arms around the girl's tempting, soft body and covered her lips with his own. Quickly, she impulsively forced herself upon George pushing him back onto the startled Faye. George found himself happily trapped. However, the impending exploration was abruptly halted by the urgent voice of the girl behind him.

"Wait a minute. What are you two trying to do? If I am in the way, please let me out."

It was then that Goerig, momentarily losing his balance, slipped on the tile floor with two naked bodies conveniently landing on top of him. Slowly untangling, the three wound up sitting with their backs against wall, laughing and gasping for breath. Finally, the private struggled to his feet, as his desires were temporarily thwarted for the time being.

"Okay, cocktail time, you dolls. Last one out is a party pooper."

George gallantly pulled the unabashed females to their feet, kissed them briefly on their cheeks, and turned off the faucets.

The girls walked shamelessly into the bedroom as their gracious host tossed them each a fresh towel.

"How about getting the first rubdown?" Goerig invitingly asked.

Faye laughed jokingly. "Oh thanks. You poor, abused Yankees are real gentlemen." She boldly walked over and began massaging George with her towel, saying, "I don't do this for just everyone. Consider yourself very lucky."

"Oh, I do!" exclaimed the private. "You'd better believe me."

The girl concentrated on drying off her accommodating host but purposely avoided the area that would rearose his manhood. George then modestly pulled on his shorts while the dolls wrapped the large towels, sarong-like, around their shapely, provocative bodies, barely able to conceal all their main points of interest. As the three laughingly paraded through the living room, the unsuspecting bell hop, Johnnie, opened the door and entered.

"Whoops!" he hollered as he turned and started to back his way into the room with a full tray in his hands and two negligees draped over one arm.

"Turn around and come on in, boy, we're decent," George said, trying to convince the embarrassed lad.

The latter blushingly placed the Scotch and accessories on the coffee table. He hesitated and then timidly handed the girls their respective flimsy night gowns. The two dolls simultaneously dropped the towels from their curvaceous figures and brazenly began slipping the transparent negligees over their heads as a very red-faced bell hop gaped incredulously.

Faye and Laverne then slowly walked over to Johnnie and each put their arms around the shaking boy and kissed him on both cheeks. Suddenly, he ducked his head and hurriedly broke away from their warm embraces and bolted for the open door.

"Hey how about your tip?" George shouted.

"Save it for later, sir. I have to go!" he yelled back as he ran down the hallway.

The three laughed as Goerig walked over to pour the long-awaited drinks.

Supper had been served. The girls had had some type of an English dish as the host settled for a filet mignon, rare.

He had put on his pajamas and the three of them were comfortably lounging on a huge sofa, slowly sipping brandies.

The two relaxed guests had been relating the story of their lives and how they happened to be in Shanghai at the time of the attack on Pearl Harbor. They recounted their terrific ordeal at the internment camp. Upon being released, they fortunately had been able to obtain passage on a comfortably English freighter, which was leaving for London in the morning.

"Well, don't oversleep and miss that trip," George warned.

"We won't," answered Faye, confidently. "I left a call down at the desk to waken us early enough. What baggage we have is already on board, and the steward is a very good friend of ours from the internment camp. Fortunately, his boat was not sunk during the recent bombings of Shanghai. He said it is in good shape and they have quite a few anxious passengers eager to get back home."

Goerig had briefly told the girls about his experiences in the China and Burma theaters of war, and they marveled at his ultimate good fortune. The evening passed too quickly.

"Don't you think it would be a good idea if we all turned in since you have to get up so early?" the private confidently asked, as though the three of them had been accustomed to sleeping together.

Faye sat up. "I think that is a jolly good idea. I'm bushed."

"I'm not bushed, just pleasantly happy right now," purred Laverne, as she snuggled her head on George's shoulder.

In the meantime, the latter tried to casually slip his hand between the vee of her gown to caress one soft and tempting breast.

Quickly, she sat up and hastily withdrew the searching hand.

"But maybe that is a good idea," reflected the girl.

The private sadly got up and walked over to the bed. He invitingly glanced at the girls as he pulled back the blanket, and laid down onto the soft contours of the mattress. Without hesitation, Faye turned out the light and the tired females climbed in, one on each side. George promptly put his arms around Laverne and pulled her unresisting body close to him. She slowly put one leg over his and whispered. "Hold me tight tonight cause I think I am going to like it."

He murmured in her ear, "You had better, baby. It's going to be a long night." Memories flickered in the back of his mind as he thought fleetingly about one night in Chungking.

After a few minutes, Faye grumbled, "George, why do I always get stuck with your back?"

He turned and put one arm around her shoulder as she laid a bare arm across his chest.

Goerig had never had it so good. But it was the soft, muffled breathing of the two dolls that soon lulled him to sleep. At least there were no creaking bed springs this time.

The private belatedly awoke with a start and looked around the room, dazedly wondering where the hell he was. The girls had gone and suddenly he felt very much alone. Reaching for the phone, he called room service and ordered up two double bloody Mary's. It was then that he noticed a note on the side table. He opened it and read,

> Dear George,
>
> We both had a wonderful evening. It couldn't have been nicer. If you ever get to London be sure and knock us up.
>
> Love, Faye and Laverne

It was several years later when it was explained to Goerig that the term "knock us up sometime" simply meant, "Call us when you are around."

Amusing people, those English. And a helluva a lot of fun.

CHAPTER TWENTY-TWO

George spent most of the morning in bed, sleeping, reading, and relishing every minute of it. About one o'clock, he got up and showered. Unfortunately, this time it had to be by himself. In the familiar confines of the shower room, he began to get aroused again, as he recalled those two pair of soft hands lathering his body. Quickly, he turned on the cold water, and his thoughts conveniently died down.

He briskly toweled himself off and got dressed in a clean suit of khakis. Noting the absence of any stripes on his sleeve, he thought, "How can anybody tell what rank I am? In fact, I could even pass for a war correspondent. Not a bad idea. Who would know the difference? Better play it by ear. I don't know what news agency I'd represent. But I always had a weak spot for the Hearst organization. Okay, Goerig, knock it off." He suddenly realized that things must be getting out of control if he is talking to himself.

After leaving his combat boots outside the door to have them shined, George opened the two-way cubicle inside the wide door and hung up his other khaki suit to be cleaned.

The phone rang. It was Johnnie.

"Mister Goerig, would you care for breakfast?"

"No thanks, boy. I'm having it now. I'll talk with you later."

Hanging up the phone, George walked over to the table and slowly measured a couple of jiggers of Scotch into a glass. He then added an equal amount of soda and quickly gulped it down. "That should do it," he figured, as he walked out the door. Coming out of the elevator he stopped by the desk to leave off his key. He found the same English clerk on duty.

"Having a jolly evening, old chap?" he inquired.

"Jolly, just jolly," Goerig quipped back.

As the private went through the main entrance out into the street, he was met by a very strange and sickening odor. It was the first time that he had noticed the large size body of flowing water about two hundred yards off to the east. It was the Huang Fu river. The stench of its sewage outflow was something he eventually got used to whether he wanted to or not.

There was a moderate stream of people on the sidewalk and the double deck buses dominated the street traffic, a multitude of trams and rickshaws. George leisurely strolled down the main avenue known as The Bund. It was as internationally known as New York's Fifth Avenue. He became aware of the tall buildings he passed. There was the Bank of China, the Customs Building, and several other medium-sized structures that occupied only one side of the street. This small sector of the city at one time comprised the heart of the financial empire of Nationalist China prior to the Japanese occupation. A playing field of sorts covered a large area next to the river. Goerig heard later that it had been a racetrack of note during Shanghai's better times. With the threatening power of the communists under Mao Tse-tung looming ominously in the West, the private wondered if China would ever revert to its former power among the Asian countries.

After a two-hour stroll, the private felt that a little libation would be good for his system, so he retraced his steps back to the hotel. Learning that the bar was conveniently located on the fourth floor, he soon found himself in a familiar position on a bar stool, which he had sorely missed the past fifteen months.

"Scotch and soda, please" was the order.

A large, ruddy-faced man with a walrus mustache placed a glass in front of George and proceeded to pour in a double jigger of Black and White Scotch. Reaching down, he brought up a seltzer bottle and expertly shot a burst of its bubbly contents to complete the drink. Lifting up a tumbler in front of him, he smiled and said, "Cheers."

"Cheers to you, sir," George answered, figuring that anyone who would serve that size of a drink must warrant being called "sir."

The bartender drained his glass. "That will be fifty cents in American currency, sir."

Goerig was stunned. "You've got to be kidding. It would be five times that much back in the States."

He quickly pulled out some Chinese notes and tossed them on the counter. Happily, he thought to himself, "This is the way to go." Little did he know that two weeks later a one-jigger drink would be two dollars. Of course, that was after the Navy hit town. "Uncle Sugar," he said to himself, "they could see you coming."

Anxiously looking forward to an evening of excitement, George casually asked the bartender if he knew of any night clubs in town where a stranger could find some female companionship and enjoy a dance or two.

Without hesitation, the man leaned over and confidentially whispered, "Chi Chi's is the best in Shanghai."

The bartender had replied so quickly, it seemed as though he must have been some kind of a public relations man for the club. Fortunately, as the private was to learn later, the man was only telling the truth.

"Where is it located?" was the next question.

"Out in the French Concession. It was a popular spot for the German and Japanese officers. You'll like it. Girls of all types and description are available." He added, "For various duties and prices, of course."

"Germans?" The private looked amazed. "Were there many of them here in Shanghai?"

The man behind the bar looked surprised and laughed. "You are sitting right in their former headquarters. This hotel was full of them. That is, until they lost their part of the war. Then the Japs kicked them out. There is a story going around about that." He paused as he took a drink to a customer sitting at the far end of the bar. After coming back, he continued,

"Well, it gives you an idea of how the Nips felt about their allies after they got beaten in Europe. It goes like this. A Japanese officer slapped his German friend on the back and said to him, 'We good friends—you will be the last we put in jail.'"

The bartender stepped back and laughed heartily at his own little story. "How about that?"

Goerig didn't appear too amused and questioned the man again.

"How far is Chi Chi's and how do I get there?"

The bartender looked slightly let down at the private's lack of response to his humor. But he perked up when he thought he could be of assistance to the American.

"Just go downstairs and get any rickshaw in front of the hotel. Just say Chi Chi's. He'll take you right there." Then he cautiously added, "But don't go paying those little bastards a lot of money. You'll spoil it for the rest of us, and it makes it hard on all of the civilians. A quarter at the most in your American money."

He then proceeded to explain to Goerig the current rate of exchange, which was around seven hundred and fifty CNC (Chinese national currency) dollars to one American dollar. He also mentioned that the rates could be very different on the black market, and the comparative rates were fluctuating daily. George thought to himself that he should have had those conniving contractors hack in Laifeng give him his three thousand dollars in American currency. Oh, hell, it's only money. Finishing his drink, he rose to go.

The bartender leaned over and gave the private some parting advice. "Have a good time but watch out for some of those girls. They're a few that aren't too clean." He winked.

"I'll be careful. Thanks for the tip, I'll remember it."

Goerig went down the elevator and through the lobby. He recalled the small package of condoms he had stashed in his barracks bag back in Kunmung. He thought they might come in handy sometime and hoped they would. It was really wonderful how Uncle Sam took such good care of his fighting men. George walked out into the street with renewed confidence. He climbed in an empty rickshaw at the curb. The Chinese driver looked at him quizzically.

"Chi Chi's" was the answer. He didn't realize it at the time but, it was a name that was to be repeated many times before he left Shanghai.

The old man reached down and picked up the bars of his vehicle and wheeled out into the slow-moving traffic. It was starting to get dark and a cool breeze seemed to stimulate his emotions as Goerig silently swore at himself. "Dammit, I should have had another double."

Following a trip that seemed very short, probably due to the interesting scenes around him, the rickshaw pulled over in front of a flickering, lighted neon sign that boldly read "Chi Chi's." George got out and paid the man what he had been told to. Then he hesitated and handed him another note. The coolie still stood with his hand out.

The private started to pet mad. "Get lost, you stinking little bastard. You're overpaid now."

The driver hurriedly picked up his rickshaw and melted away into the street. George looked around for the entrance to the night club. It was an uphill walk. He eagerly took the steps two at a time in his anxiousness to see where all the music was coming from, which could be heard down out on the sidewalk. As he reached the top of the stairs, he stopped and looked around, amazed. Could this be for real? It was strictly stateside, with the exception of the mixed variety of patrons.

There was a majority of Caucasians along with Chinese, turbaned Indians, and even a few black men. George started to go past the bar leading to the dance floor and the reserved tables. The bar extended approximately seventy feet alongside one wall of the night club. Suddenly, he stopped again and gaped incredulously at the assorted female clientele occupying every stool.

The bevy of heavily rouged faces with dark scared eyes and crimson red lips looked expectantly at the startled American. Tight-fitting Chinese dresses, slit up one side and exposing a wide expanse of pink fleshy, momentarily distracted him from the upper portions of their bodies.

Breasts of every type and size seemed to be competing with each other in their own private battle of the bulge. George was amazed at the uninhibited display of wanton female sex spread out before his eyes. He again hesitated and thought to himself, "George, you can do better than this."

Knowing it he had to pass through a gauntlet of hardened femininity in order to reach the section of the club with tables, the private took a deep breath and bravely started down the narrow aisle. The entire row of chattering females quickly became alert as they all turned to critically appraise the blushing American.

Their pointed invitations were short and brazenly crude.

"Hi Yank, busy tonight?"

"Want some fun?"

"Me hot for all you."

Goerig ignored them all as he finally reached the last overly made-up dame. Suddenly she thrust an enticing leg across his path, forcing him to stop.

He looked at her and slowly began getting angry.

"Knock it off, baby, I'm here on business."

She laughed. "So am I. Why don't we make a deal together? I've got a good proposition."

George quickly slapped her leg down and moved on.

"Yank bastard," she spat after him.

The private heaved a sigh of relief as he approached a short and haughty-looking maître d'. He was Chinese and the situation reminded Goerig of some of the Oriental afterhours night clubs in Seattle.

"Table for two, sir?"

The private looked behind to see if there was anyone with him. There was nobody.

"No, no. I'm strictly by myself."

The small, self-important man drew himself up and contemptuously said, "Sorry sir, couples, only."

George looked down at the Oriental incredulously and quickly grabbed him by his coat lapels. "Why you little slant-eyed bastard! I am an American soldier. I've been fighting for your stinking country. I want a good table now and I want it fast."

The seated groups next to them had stopped their conversations and were expectantly waiting to see the outcome of the interesting and suddenly heated one-sided conversation.

The startled, intimidated, and shaking maître d' accommodatingly bowed.

"After me, sir."

As he led the American across the dance floor, Goerig noticed a group of several rough-looking characters who were in the midst of a lively party. When Goerig started to pass their table, a tall, husky-built negro stood up and looked at him.

"Hey, man, I'll bet y'all are from the States. Right?" Without waiting for an answer, he continued, "So are we—Merchant Marines. Caught by the little Jap bastards when the war broke out. Been in a f-----g internment camp ever since. How about joining us?"

George paused. and under the dire need of wanting to be alone, he graciously begged off. "Got a date, man. First in a long time. How about some other night?"

The colored sailor quickly answered, "Hell yes. We'd like some dates ourselves. We might even have to finally wind up with some of those pigs over there at the bar. That is, if they don't want too much of that green stuff. We ain't been paid all our dough as yet." He waved the private on. "See you later, alligator."

The temporary interest at the table lessened as George's reason for rejection of their offer seemed to be accepted.

The maître d' drew back a chair at a table for two and briskly removed the reservation card placed on the linen covered top.

"Is this satisfactory, sir?"

"It will do," Goerig crisply answered, as he slipped a couple of notes in the outstretched hand. The man didn't realize it at the time, but eventually the private was going to be one of his better customers.

George was surprised as an English waiter came up to his table. "What would you care to have, sir?"

"A double Scotch and soda, please" was the reply.

"Right away, sir."

Goerig leaned back in his chair, relishing the idea of being called "sir." He slowly scanned the happy, boisterous crowd, with their ice-tinkling glasses playing a beautiful serenade to his ears.

"Oh, man, this is it," he thought. "It's been a long, long time, but now, you lucky boy, you finally made it. If only Captain Paine could see you sitting here."

He looked over towards the bar and wondered what his former commanding officer in Burma would have done with one of those floozies. Probably wound up with a "dose." Realistically, though, he couldn't be that dumb. However, if it would have happened, what the hell, it couldn't have happened to a nicer bastard. His brief reverie was momentarily interrupted by the dignified waiter as the man placed his drink on his table.

The latter hesitated to see his customer's reactions as he took a sip of the tepid liquor. George looked at him disdainfully.

"Where the hell is the ice? I asked for a double. This thing is really a farce. Take it back and put some more Scotch in it too." He looked angrily at the man as the he hesitated. "I'll pay for it, damn it. Get your ass going!"

The waiter apologized. "There is no ice, sir. But I will have the bartender put some more Scotch in your drink," he hastily added as he picked up the glass.

Goerig then recalled that the English did not care for ice in their drinks. However, to each his own. Tonight was his night.

While waiting for the waiter to return, he idly glanced around the room at the tables, which were placed on elevated tiers, conveniently providing an ample view of the dance floor.

"Wonder if they have any floor shows?" the private silently muttered to himself. Again he looked at the happy, noisy crowd, each person in it searching for somebody special. Suddenly, his roving eyes abruptly stopped as he concentrated on one of the raised tables.

Behind it sat a handsome young man holding hands with a beautiful blonde girl. They were intently gazing at each other, oblivious to their surroundings and seemingly enrapt in their own thoughts.

George came to a quick conclusion. This is what he had been looking for. The waiter, in the meantime, had returned to the table.

"Bring me another one, double. Don't forget," the American ordered.

The waiter again hesitated as he gaped unbelievingly at the private while the latter thirstily downed the Scotch and soda in two gulps.

Goerig stood up. "If I'm not here when you get back, bring my glass up to that table over there, where that lovely couple holding hands is sitting." He pointed in the general direction of his objective. Then, slipping some more Chinese notes into the man's eager, waiting hand, George pushed back his chair and confidently started to wend his way through the crowded tables.

Approaching the young couple George began, "I am sorry to intrude, but I am a stranger here in your city. Do you mind if I join you?"

The startled pair looked up at the uninvited intruder in amazement. Then, quickly, the young man rose and extended his hand.

"Not at all. My name is Boris Olienakov. This is my wife, Irene. We would be happy to have you join us."

The sudden friendliness and the excellent English with which the man had greeted Goerig were wonderful, unexpected surprises.

Goerig paused momentarily before saying, "Thank you. My name is George Goerig. I am a private in the American Air Force. I was hoping to find somebody with whom I could share the evening. Are you sure I am not intruding?"

The disarming smile convinced the private of the man's sincerity.

Unintentionally, George stared at the gorgeous creature sitting in front of him. Her hair was silken blond and draped down over alabaster white, strapless shoulders and shimmered under an overhead light. Her eyes were a pale blue and strikingly alert. The warm glow of her pink cheeks radiated as her moist, red lips opened slightly.

"We would love to have you with us," she said softly.

Entranced, George groped for the empty chair and sat down.

"Boris, your wife is beautiful."

He laughed. "Now words like that coming from an American is a real nice compliment. Isn't it, dear?"

She smiled. "Wonderful, thank you. I like you already."

Boris unintentionally interrupted the temporary spell that had overcome his guest.

"What are you drinking?"

Goerig looked at his newfound friends as he felt slightly embarrassed by the obvious attention he had shown Irene. Boris was obviously not the jealous type, though, and had probably gotten used to his wife turning heads.

"I believe the waiter is going to bring my drink up here to your table. I was hoping to be invited and I took the liberty of telling him to do so. I don't want you to think that I'm being too presumptuous."

"Not at all, not at all!" Boris exclaimed. Changing the subject, he asked, "Where is your home in America?"

"Seattle, Washington," Goerig replied. "Do you know where that is?"

"Yes, very well. The knowledge of geography of the United States is one of the most important phases in our educational system. Of course, the understanding of your language is one of the major factors we must start learning, when we are young." The young Russian continued, "You might have suspected, which is true, that Irene and I are white Russians. Both of our parents fled their mother country when the communists overran the Tsar's army in 1917. They were very fortunate to have escaped with their lives. We were both born in Harbin, Manchuria, before our folks moved to Shanghai, quite a few years ago." He paused to take a sip of his drink. "We have a large community of white Russians living in the French Concession. We like it very much, don't we dear?"

Boris turned to his wife and kissed her tenderly on the cheek. She returned the kiss and then resumed the conversation where her husband had left off.

"Boris and I were both fortunate enough to be able to go to a school which had American teachers. They helped us tremendously in mastering your English language."

George temporarily interrupted. "You are both perfect as far as I am concerned. How many languages do you speak?"

Irene locked quizzically at her husband for a moment, then turned back to the private.

"I speak four, but Boris can speak six languages."

Her husband smiled and explained his linguistic advantage over his wife. "George, I am a food broker, and it is important to my business that I am able to converse with all my customers and produce merchants in their native language." He then started to number off on his fingers. "Russian and Chinese, naturally. Then English, French, German." He hesitated and smiled. "Maybe a little Spanish, since we deal with the Filipinos also."

"No Latin?" George jokingly asked. "Why, back home, the Catholic school I attended required us to take four years of Latin, and I've yet to meet an ancient Roman who I can practice on."

The three laughed and Goerig could sense that a warm feeling of mutual comradeship had sprung up between them. Hesitatingly, he looked over to Boris and frankly asked, "How long have you two been married, if I'm not being too personal?"

"All of three months. In fact, tonight, we are celebrating our anniversary. You might even say that we are still newlyweds, wouldn't you?"

"I certainly would," George replied.

The music from the mixed members of the six-piece orchestra started playing again. The song was Cole Porter's "Night and Day," George's favorite.

Eagerly, he rose from the table and politely asked Boris. "Pardon me, but may I please dance with your wife? It has been such a long time since I have danced."

The husband looked over at his wife and smiled. "Would you like to dance with George?"

"I would love to, if you promise that you will miss me," she answered.

"I'll try not to."

George got up, pulled Irene's chair back in gentlemanly fashion, took her hand, and escorted her down to the dance floor. It was starting to get crowded as Goerig gently placed his hand around her slender waist and the two moved gracefully out between the dancing couples. The girl's rhythm was flawless and she felt as light as a feather.

The American whispered in her ear, "Pardon me if it takes me a little while to get used to dancing again."

She drew back her head a little to look him in the eye. "What do you mean? You are a wonderful dancer. I won't say you are better than my husband, but you are just as good."

Goerig smiled gently at her. "That's all I wanted to hear."

They danced to two pieces, and George felt he could go on forever when Irene finally whispered, "Don't you think we should go back and join Boris? I have never left him alone for so long." As they parted, she added, "I did enjoy dancing with you. We'll do it again soon, I hope."

The two reached the table. Boris stood up, and as he seated his wife, he murmured in her ear. Irene quickly nodded her head and said, "Of course, she would be just the one for George. Why didn't I think of that?"

The private suddenly became very interested in Irene's remark to her husband.

"What gives?" he asked. His curious expression did not belie his expectant hopes. "Are you going to get me fixed up with a date?"

"Her name is Maria and you will love her. I think she is just the one for you," Irene answered and then continued, "She is twenty years old and was Miss Shanghai this past year."

"Miss Shanghai?" Goerig's eyes widened. "You must be kidding. How could there have been beauty contests here with the Japs in charge of everything?"

Boris leaned over and put his hand on the private's knee. "George, they did not run everything. You would be surprised. They wanted us to maintain our normal way of life. They wanted our cooperation. Russia was not at war with the Japanese government until near the end of hostilities. Maria won the contest last year. I am sure we can arrange a date for you with her. Fortunately, she and Irene are close friends."

His wife confidently carried on the conversation, saying, "I know she would, love it. Maria has always said that she would like to go out with an American, when the war was over. She went to school at a convent here in Shanghai run by American Maryknoll nuns." Irene added, "That girl is not only beautiful; she is also very smart with a wonderful personality. I am sure you will love her."

George could hardly wait for the blonde girl to finish. "Okay, I'm sold. When do I meet her?"

"When would you like to? Tomorrow evening?" answered Boris. He hesitated. "That is, if she isn't busy."

"The sooner the better. I'm ready." Goerig's long-dormant emotions were starting to get the better of him.

Eventually, the evening had to come to an end. It was too soon as far as the American was concerned. It had been perfect. He silently marveled at the fact that he had been so fortunate in meeting such a lovely couple as those two. As they parted on the sidewalk outside the darkened nightclub, Boris shook George's hand, and Irene softly kissed him on the cheek.

"Tomorrow night, then? I gave you the address where to meet us. We'll see you about eight o'clock."

"Eight o'clock, it is," Goerig confirmed. "I will be looking forward to it. Good night and pleasant dreams."

They separated as the private hailed an empty rickshaw and tiredly climbed in.

"Parke Hotel, *quidi, quidi.*"

The boy nodded understandingly and they were on their way down the empty street. The rhythmic sound of his padding feet and the slight swaying of the two-wheeled vehicle soon lulled George to sleep. It wasn't long, though, before the rickshaw drew up in front of the hotel.

"Pok hotel, Pok hotel," the coolie jabbered.

"I hear you, I hear you," Goerig drowsily answered as he practically fell out on the street. Handing the boy some notes and really not caring how much, he proceeded to stumble over the curb and head for the imposing doors of his hotel. He hoped he could make it up to his room as his brain was not focusing too well. What a hangover! Never again! Till the next time.

CHAPTER TWENTY-THREE

The sun's rays were trying to burst through the closed drapes of his room, and as George rolled over, he quietly moaned, "Too much, too quick."

He blindly groped for the phone on the side table, where he thought it might be. It wasn't there. Instead of going to the bother and pain of sitting up, he grabbed the cord as the instrument noisily clattered to the floor. Slowly pulling it towards him, he managed to get it to his ear. He was greeted by a cheery, "Good morning, Good morning. How are you this fine morning, Mister Goerig?"

"Lousy, if you don't mind. Have Johnnie bring me up some Alka-Seltzer and two wild cows."

The voice on the other end hesitated. "Two wild cows?" he asked in a perplexed tone.

The private irritatingly hollered at the man's unintentional ignorance.

"Wild cows. Moose milk? Call it what you want. Oh hell, send me up a bottle of Scotch, a quart of milk, and some honey. That'll do it. I'll make my own."

"Yes sir, coming right up, sir" was the bewildered reply.

When the rap came on the door, George managed to shout, "Come on in. The door is unlocked, I think."

His new friend and self-appointed buddy, Johnnie, came in with a loaded tray and set it down on the table. He then walked over to the wide picture windows and started to draw the drapes.

"Leave those damn curtains closed till I'm ready. Bring the tab over here," Goerig ordered.

He hastily scrawled his name on the chit. "There's some money on the table. Don't get greedy. There'll be more. Just help yourself to a normal tip and close the door softly on your way out. Don't bang it. My head is killing me."

As he heard the door shut, George put his feet over the side of the bed and unsteadily moved toward the table.

He pondered over the sudden decision he had to make so early in the morning. "What should I take first?"

He picked up one of the Chinese coins laying on the table.

"Heads, an Alka-Seltzer. Tails a wild cow."

He flipped the coin in the air and clumsily missed it as it bounced off the ceiling. Looking down at the coin on the floor, he squinted at the side features and declared, "Heads." George reached for the Scotch and the quart of milk. He then proceeded to make himself a wild cow.

The private sighed. "Oh well, you can't win them all."

As he sat back down on the bed, Goerig began to rationalize that he could not sleep all afternoon and be real sharp when it came time to meet his blind date. He finished his first drink and slowly began to achieve another warm glow. After the third one, he laid back and slept peaceably till late afternoon. When he finally awoke, George fixed himself the belated Alka-Seltzer.

After managing to get most of it down, he suddenly rushed to the bathroom. Following a few minutes, he emerged, feeling a little lighter and delighted in the fact that his big stomach seemed happier. Walking over to the door's cubicle, he removed his freshly laundered and pressed khaki shirt and pants. Fortunately, the private was not bothered by having to make a difficult decision about which outfit to wear that night.

The same procedure was enacted every day, making Goerig the cleanest and smartest dressed GI in Shanghai. However, at the time he did not realize he was the only GI in town, no less.

The address Boris had given him was in the French Concession. It was predominantly comprised of white Russians. As he approached his objective and rechecked the number on the avenue, he was mildly surprised to find the address was a walk-up apartment, above a jewelry store. He had yet to visit any residential districts in town but was pleased that his immediate places of interest were not too far from the Parke Hotel. That included Chi Chi's, which was in the vicinity of the Russian's apartment.

As he rang the doorbell at the street entrance, a head leaned out of the window directly above him. It was Boris.

"Come on up. I'll press the buzzer."

An electrical hum indicated that the door was unlocked.

George opened it and started to climb the carpet-covered stairs. Irene was waiting for him at the top of the landing.

"Welcome to our humble abode," she said, laughing melodiously. "You finally found us. Did you have any difficulty?"

Goerig clasped her hand and kissed her lightly on her soft, dimpled check.

"If you had told me you lived so close to Chi Chi's, I could have been here sooner. I'm quickly starting to learn my way around Shanghai. I can direct the rickshaw on a straighter course. Does that make sense?"

"If you say so, I will agree."

Their apartment was very small. Quickly glancing around, George noticed a kitchenette off the living room. An open door revealed a double bed, which occupied most of the space in the bedroom. A bureau of drawers and a dressing table fitted snugly to one side. He was about to mention that the entire apartment could fit nicely in the living room of his hotel suite. However, for obvious reasons, he refrained.

Boris walked out of the kitchen and shook his guest's hand. "You are in luck. Maria had a date with this fellow she has been going out with, but she broke it when we told her about you. It was with some rich fellow she wasn't too interested in anyway. Jealous man, but harmless."

The private thought to himself, "That's all I need is a jealous boyfriend." Fortunately, since it would have spoiled his evening, he did not know at the time that the jealous boyfriend was going to resort to some drastic action later on regarding the health of one said private.

Boris continued, "We are to pick her up at her apartment in about a half an hour. It is just down the street. Would you care for a drink before we leave?"

"Love one," George replied, trying to disguise his eagerness to warm up to the occasion before meeting his blind date.

The genial host came in with two glasses in his hands, explaining that Irene drank very little and that he usually handled the vodka consumption in the family. As Goerig's anxiety mounted, Boris quickly finished his drink, and Irene emerged from the bedroom with gloves in her hand. She had on a beige coat with a small mink collar.

"Ready?" she asked.

"Never been readier," was the answer.

The streetlights had been turned on, and a few pedestrians were window shopping as they strolled along the avenue.

After a few blocks, Boris stopped and said, "Well, here we are."

They were standing in front of a cobbler shop, as the sign on the plate glass window indicated. Irene told George that it was owned by Maria's father. The entrance to her apartment was adjacent and similar to the one they had just left.

The private began to feel butterflies in his stomach. "Should have had another drink to kill these little bastards," he thought to himself.

A window opened above them as George temporarily panicked. He had tucked his service cap over his small balding spot on the top of his head, which was clearly visible to the girl looking down on him. He resignedly figured she might as well know the worse. He could always rely on his outstanding personality, if need be. "Confidence, boy."

"Please come up" was the invitation.

As the three climbed the steps and entered the apartment, they were met by Maria's parents. Boris introduced his new friend. They seemed pleased to meet the young American. Their last name was Rostov. A few words were politely exchanged in Russian as Goerig patiently waited for his date to come out from one of the rooms.

The apartment was similar to the Olienakovs' but had an additional bedroom and the living room seemed a little larger.

Finally, a bright, cheerful voice announced the appearance of George's date. The girl was radiantly beautiful. A broad smile displayed a row of perfect glistening teeth there were nevertheless overshadowed by two sparkling large brown eyes. Her long dark hair was smoothly combed back over her shoulders and slightly danced at the shake of her head. With a flawless complexion and the warm glow of her dimpled cheeks, Goerig was left breathless.

Irene did the long-awaited honors. "George, meet Maria. Maria, this is George."

She extended a welcoming hand. The private didn't know whether to kiss it or clasped it, so he merely held on to it and continued to gaze at the exquisite and wonderous doll.

Meanwhile, she approvingly looked at both Boris and Irene, as her new date was becoming engrossed in a manner that was starting to be embarrassing. Finally, George recovered his tongue.

"It is a real pleasure. I'm sure we are going to have a wonderful evening."

Maria beamed. "Where do we go tonight?"

Goerig hesitatingly asked, "Do you like dancing?"

"I love it. Sometimes, I feel I could dance all night. And you?" she replied.

"I'm your boy then. I know we are going to have a good time. Shall we be on our way?"

George looked over at his approving friends, who seemingly happy about the match they had just made.

"How about Chi Chi's again? I enjoyed their music and the place is close." He then hesitated a moment. "That is, unless you had some other plans in mind."

"Chi Chi's it is," confirmed Boris. "Let us be on our way."

Goerig dutifully went over to Maria's parents as he noticed that their apprehension about their daughter's first date with an American had seemed to vanish.

He warmly shook their hands and told them he had enjoyed their company. Mrs. Rostov had started to tell the young man to be sure and have her daughter home early when Maria quickly interrupted with a few chosen Russian words. Her mother quickly stopped and just smiled. The father, whose weather lined face betrayed his age, merely nodded, assuming they had nothing to worry about as long as Boris and Irene were along. How right they were.

As the four reached the sidewalk, George slipped his arm inside of Maria's and happily escorted her in the general direction of the night club. The preoccupied newlyweds followed close behind, lost in their own little world.

The men were checking the girl's coats at the hat room, as the latter had left to go to the powder salon.

"Well?" asked the host.

"Oh man!" Goerig exclaimed. "Where has she been all my life? As if I didn't know. As far as I'm concerned, Boris, she could have been Miss America. Man, she is beautiful. I can't thank you enough."

The Russian looked at his friend skeptically. "Perhaps someday . . ." he said, then paused. "Perhaps someday I may ask a favor of you in the near future, and maybe that will even things up."

Having a faint idea of what his host was thinking about, George hastily replied, "Anything. You name it and if I am in a position to help you out, Boris, I'll certainly try and do it."

At this point, the girls returned. and the foursome headed for the maitre d's station. As they passed the bar, it was apparent that the hustling whores had not achieved their objectives, yet, for the night. They seemed to be engrossed with the activities of two burley bartenders. George felt like mischievously pinching the fanny of the whore who had called him a bastard. Wisely, he refrained. It was not the time or places to create a scene. That was to come later.

The maitre d's was standing by his golden rope, which barred the so-called undesirables from entering into his inner sanctum. However, when he saw Boris, his haughty expression relaxed quickly and quickly changed into a broad smile. He bowed.

"Welcome, Mister Olienakov. The same table, yes?"

Boris calmly nodded his head and indicated he wanted two more chairs for his guests.

The Chinese manager then noticed the American private. His mouth dropped open in surprise. However, he quickly regained his composure and unclasped his restraining golden rope. He then led the two couples across the empty dance floor.

The small tables were rapidly filling up. The stares of nearby patrons, combined with hushed conversations and the nods of their heads, indicated a positive appraisal of the young foursome. George had, indeed, been very fortunate. As soon as they were seated, Boris immediately put his arm around his wife and kissed her on the cheek. "I love you," he murmured.

"I love you too," she answered.

George looked at Maria as she winked and said, "Don't worry about it, I've been putting up with this for the past six months, and finally I just ignore it."

"What would you care to drink?" Goerig ventured.

She hesitated and then asked him what he was going to have.

"Scotch and soda, my old standby. But no doubles tonight." He laughed.

"Doubles? Why doubles? Aren't singles strong enough for you?" she innocently asked.

"Strictly for false courage, my dear," George replied, then added, "and to get in the proper mood. But tonight, I don' t believe that the extra drinks are going to be required. I have you with me."

He started to pat her knee reassuringly, then thought better of it and wisely withdrew his hand. She might think her date was getting extremely fresh so early in the evening. That could never happen. Why, the very idea!

The orchestra was tuning their instruments and, after a short pause, began to play. It was "Begin the Beguine," George's all-time favorite. He looked over to see a pair of expectant, shining eyes and anxiously asked, "Now?"

"Now," the radiant doll answered as she pushed back her chair before her companion could reach for it. She impatiently started to lead the way down to the dance floor. It was practically empty as the fast-moving strains of the orchestra had discouraged a large portion of the drinking patrons.

The tantalizing aroma of an exotic perfume enticed George's senses as he gently took the girl in his arms and they slowly floated out on the floor. After the first few steps, George realized he had a Russian Ginger Rogers in his arms, only twice as beautiful.

They twirled together and Goerig tried every intricate step he had ever associated with the familiar melodies of Cole Porter. Maria followed him perfectly as though they were one. He softly whispered in her ear, "Where did you ever learn to dance like this?"

As she drew hack her head from his shoulder, George became perturbed with himself for disrupting the closeness of her warm body.

The girl impishly grinned. "I'll never tell."

Her flushed face shone and only added to her beautiful features. George tenderly pulled her back to him and whispered again, "I can believe it."

The tone of the music rapidly rose to a crescendo and ended with the closing lyric of "when they begin the beguine." Private Goerig was in paradise.

CHAPTER TWENTY-FOUR

For three glorious weeks, Boris, Irene, Maria, and George had become a close-knit foursome. It seemed as though they had known each other for years. Goerig found himself growing deeply attached to the vibrant, young, attractive girl, who needed to speak only one language when she was with him, as she also had to speak Russian and Chinese. It wasn't long before their eyes were expressing something of a warmer nature.

One special night, Maria suggested that just the two of them visit a small restaurant owned by a friend of her father. He hastily agreed and then slyly mentioned he would love to go anywhere with her.

"America?" she jokingly asked.

George quickly changed the subject.

Their primary mode of transportation had been the pedicab. It consisted of a bicycle-powered vehicle similar to the horse-drawn hansoms very common to New York's Central Park. They also provided a cozy situation where Goerig could put his arm around Maria and try to say the things George had to constantly remind himself of things he shouldn't have—that he was still very much in love with the girl he had left behind in the States. Despite his extracurricular activities, which he thought was a necessity for his virile nature, the American was not about to let himself be carried away. However, it was a very strong temptation at a time when he was quite vulnerable.

On that warm, delightful evening, following a half hour's ride to the northern sector of the city, they arrived at a small but conspicuous restaurant, conspicuous because it had Russian and English signs emblazoned on its red brick façade. Goerig helped Maria down from her seat and paid off the old wizened driver, who had amazed him with his enduring performance on peddling the bicycle.

The two entered a narrow doorway as the melodic strains of a violin reached their ears. Inside, the interior design gave forth a warm and comfortable feeling. George was instantly enthralled with his date's preference of restaurant for the evening.

Suddenly, an older, heavy set, but very enthused Russian rushed over towards the pair. He threw his arms around Maria and kissed her tenderly on both cheeks.

"Maria, Maria, my little babushka! Where have you been?"

He then stepped back and carefully scrutinized her companion. "Who is your friend?" he asked in a deep and resonant voice.

"Nicholas, I want you to meet George Goerig. He is with the American Air Force." For his benefit, she added, "We are good friends."

The stranger boomed, "Any friend of Maria's is a friend of mine. Welcome!"

The private's hand was engulfed in a vise-like grip, and he tried to conceal the pain from a crushing he hoped would not leave permanent injury.

"Very glad to meet you, sir," George sighed as the man released his hand.

"Come, I give you the best table in my humble place."

Nicholas led them through a maze of small tables with red and white checkered cloths lending a cheerful atmosphere to the cozy setting. Stopping at a secluded nook in the rear of the cafe, he motioned for the couple to sit down.

"This is a real special occasion. You must try our finest champagne." He leaned over to whisper in the American's ear. "It is as you people say, 'on the house.'" The genial host then quickly straightened up and bellowed, "Ivan!"

A harassed but smiling waiter came rushing over to the table with menus. As the owner turned to leave, he thoughtfully suggested, "George, let Maria do the ordering. She knows what is best."

Goerig leaned back on the bench, assured he was in good hands. "Honey, I guess you are the boss. You heard what the man said. Consider me your obedient slave."

The girl smiled. "I'll try my best to please you and cater to your desires." Then she quickly added. "For supper, that is."

The meal was sumptuous, and as the violin player approached their table, Maria requested a special tune in her native language.

The tuxedoed musician bowed and softly moved his bow over the violin. With agile fingers moving deftly on the strings, he began to play what seemed to George to be a sad rendition of a funeral dirge.

Maria's face relaxed as she became enthralled with the melodious strains. After a short while, she leaned over and whispered, "It is a Russian love song. Do you like it?"

Her date nodded his head dubiously, and with a resigned expression on his face, decided that he better like it.

After the violinist had finished and they were slowly sipping black Russian coffee, George noticed a husky, burley man approaching their table. His eyes were intently glaring at the American with unconcealed hatred. He stopped next to Maria and began speaking gruffly to her in Russian.

The girl's face reddened as she answered him in an angry tone. He reached for her arm. The private gallantly rose and laid a resisting hand on the man's shoulder.

The enraged intruder immediately stepped toward the American and wildly threw a swinging blow. Goerig ducked easily as Maria shrieked for help.

Nicholas, followed by two muscular waiters, quickly appeared on the scene, grabbed the belligerent visitor by his arms, and pinned them behind his back. He was roughly led out of the dinning sector and down some steps, screaming meanwhile in his native tongue over his shoulder. The astounded diners sitting around the embarrassed couple had stopped eating.

With sympathetic glances, they looked at Maria. She was crying and the tears were beginning to roll down her flushed cheeks. George quietly moved over to console her.

Nicholas returned to the table, still shaking with rage at the unfortunate incident. He bowed towards the two and began apologizing profusely for the belligerent actions of his obnoxious customer.

Maria slowly raised her head and sobbingly murmured, "I am terribly sorry, George. That was the man I broke an engagement with to go out with you. He is awfully jealous. I should have known better than to have you embarrassed this way."

Boris tried to explain, "Please do not worry. I know the man well. He has been drinking. I had him taken downstairs, where I will keep him till morning. I am really sorry again for what has happened. Please try and enjoy yourselves."

Goerig thanked his host and then quietly suggested he should take Maria home. He reached for his wallet to pay for the drinks and supper. Nicholas moved forward and placed a restraining hand on his arm.

"No, I refuse to take your money. Please consider yourselves as my guest." He graciously added, "I want you to come here again soon, and I assure you of a happier evening."

Still upset and angry at what had happened, the Russian leaned forward. "You will not be subjected to such crazy doings as you saw tonight."

Maria reached for her purse and gloves. The two rose from the table and slowly made their way back through the crowded dining room and then out under a starlit sky. A full moon looked down on them and seemed to express its sympathy to the young couple. George hailed a passing pedicab and they climbed in. The tear-stained face of his lovely doll nestled closely on her escort's shoulder.

It had been two days since George had last seen Maria. He had repeatedly tried to contact her, but the girl's mother claimed she was not home. Dejectedly, he later stopped by Boris's apartment to talk with Irene. The latter was very understanding and consoling as she tried to explain.

"Maria is still very upset about what occurred the other night. She is afraid to go out with you because of what Ivan might do. She will not see him again and she is afraid he might try to harm you. George," she pleaded, "please be careful. That man becomes crazy sometimes."

The determined private stubbornly persisted. "But I have to see Maria. I just can't stop being with her just because of that lunatic. I'm still a member of the United States Armed Forces. Seriously, he would have to be completely nuts to try and bother me anymore."

As it was, Goerig's wishful thinking was a bit premature. He was definitely not prepared for the unpleasant encounter that was to happen shortly. Finally, he thanked Irene and left.

Climbing into the pedicab, the private, by chance, recalled the first night at Chi Chi's when he had politely rejected the friendly invitation offered by the black Merchant Marine.

As George rode down the few blocks to the popular night club, he looked forward expectantly to meeting with the seaman again. After paying off the coolie driver, the private started up the steps to the foyer. It was approximately nine o'clock. Briefly, he glanced around the rapidly filling dining room and finally noticed the tall negro as he rose up from his chair.

"Hey, Yankee, over here," the latter yelled as he invitingly waved his arm.

George hesitantly approached the crowded table. He was met with an outstretched, welcoming hand.

"For starters, man, what the hell is your name? Mine's Joe."

"George Goerig," was the quick response. Pausing, he then added, "Private, that is."

Looking around at his fellow drinkers, the man guffawed. "Hey, how about that? A private no less. I didn't think they made those anymore."

Then, presumptuously, he put a massive arm around George's shoulder and proceeded to introduce him to his seated companions. They, in turn, nodded their heads as Goerig sat down in an empty chair. The exuberant host raised his glass and happily announced, "Today, we got our back pay. It's our last night in this stinking' town and we're going to have a ball. Here's to yuh, private. What the hell are you drinking?'"

George hesitantly glanced around the table, then asked, "How about me buying a round?"

The answer came fast. "To hell with that, man, you're our guest." The black man then waved a fistful of Chinese currency above his head. "We got the green stuff! This is our treat."

Realizing that any further argument was useless, George relaxed back in his chair. Casually, he looked around at the noisy crowd happily enjoying themselves in the smoke-filled room. Suddenly, his eyes fell upon the slightly familiar face of one belligerent-looking man sitting at the bar. He was accompanied by two other rugged individuals who appeared to be just as hostile. The three were intently glaring back at the private. The latter's expression quickly turned to one of genuine alarm. He murmured to himself, "Oh no. It's that same bastard."

"What's that you said, man?" Joe asked curiously.

"Oh nothing," George replied.

The sudden changed, frightened look on his face must have alerted his black friend as the latter slowly followed the private's gaze toward the trio sitting at the bar.

Joe concernedly asked, "You got troubles, boy?"

In view of the fact that he was hopelessly outnumbered, Goerig turned and said, "Frankly, yes, I do." He paused and then continued. "And it looks like I'm going to have a lot more."

His colored host nodded in Ivan's direction. "You all mean those boys sitting over there?"

George hesitated, then wisely decided to confide his worst fears to his new friend. "It seems that short, husky guy does not like the idea of my busting up his one-sided affair with a certain girl here in town. I managed to get out of one scrape with him, but I'm not too sure about getting out of this one. It looks like he has a couple of his friends with him tonight. This could be rough."

Joe reassuringly patted his white guest on the shoulder. "Don't you worry, man. You've got a lot of buddies right here."

Briefly, he glanced around the table. The "buddies," who had naturally overheard the short conversation, seemed to have acquired a sudden interest in the welfare of this worried GI.

"I sure hope so, cause I'm going to need all the help I can get," the worried private soberly answered.

The tall colored man turned to the rest of his attentive group and briskly announced, "Well, you heard what the man said. He needs a little help."

Joe leaned over and softly whispered in George's ear, "They won't start anything up here. You wait a few minutes after we've left and then follow us out. We'll be waiting for those cats downstairs. Now, don't you worry about a gawd-damn thing."

The five seamen casually finished the remainder of their drinks and, tossing some loose change on the table, rose from their seats and determinedly walked out in single file. They purposely ignored the overzealous prostitutes at the bar who were futiley trying to advertise their charms.

Goerig slowly finished his drink and then, nonchalantly rising, he started walking toward the exit sign lettered on the wall. Without haste, he proceeded to walk down the long staircase to the street. Upon reaching the bottom, he stepped out on a darkened sidewalk. Somebody had conveniently switched off the blinking marquee sign. Glancing to his right and left, the private became aware of his newfound friends lined up against the wall on both sides of the club's entrance. George quickly motioned to move out into the street. As soon as he did, he heard the ominous sound of pounding feet coming down the steps.

As the first figure emerged, a powerful downward blow caught the man directly on the back of his neck, sending him sprawling unconsciously on the sidewalk. The second two men, realizing they were falling into an unexpected trap, tried to stem the momentum of their rush. Unable to do so, they found themselves on the sidewalk, surrounded by five very rugged and intent seamen. George purposely turned his head away from the brutality. He didn't want to be a witness to the one-sided melee he knew was coming.

Within seconds, it was all over and two more inert bodies were unceremoniously thrown out into the gutter.

Joe turned to the private and put out his hand. "It was a pleasure, George. But I think we'd better get our asses out of here." He looked up and down the avenue. "We don't want to get mixed up with the law. I still plan on getting home to Seattle soon."

"Seattle?" George hollered in genuine surprise. "Hell, that's my hometown! Why didn't you say so before? I went to Seattle Prep. I'll bet you went to Garfield High School. Most of the colored guys did."

An amazed look slowly crossed Joe's face as he shook his head in disbelief and finally answered, "Yeah, man, played football under the old fox, Brigham, class of thirty five."

The private began to laugh. "Walter Screeching was our coach. Why, hell, we played you guys down at Washington Park in a practice game before our regular season began. I was the quarterback. One hundred and forty-five pounds."

The tall man chuckled. "So you were the little man we beat the hell out of. Them were the days."

Then, quickly, he looked again up the street to see if any police were in the vicinity. Satisfied, he grabbed George's arm, and they made their way through a quickly gathering crowd of curious onlookers.

"Come on, man, I know a spot down the street where you and I can talk over old times. I ain't goin' to miss any of this."

The low wail of a distant siren broke the silence of the night as the two disappeared around a nearby corner.

═

The following afternoon, Goerig quickly scanned the Shanghai newspaper, which now could be printed without Japanese censorship. On the second page, a small caption caught his eye.

THREE MEN BRUTALLY ASSAULTED BY UNKNOWN ASSAILANTS

He read on. It listed some of the injuries inflicted upon the innocent victims during a street fight outside of Chi Chi's night club in the French Concession. They included one broken neck, two concussions, eight cracked ribs, two fractured arms, and multiple contusions over face and body. It also noted that an open switch blade had been found in the gutter next to one of the unconscious bodies.

George unknowingly shivered as he broke out in a cold sweat and his hands began to shake. He thought about how he could have been the victim. What would have been his eventual fate if he had tried to ward off three attackers, one with a switch blade?

He decided not to call Maria. In fact he did not want anyone to know he was involved in the unfortunate incident. Goerig was, however, curious to find out the girl's reaction to what had happened to her former boyfriend, who was hurt in the fight. He wouldn't bring himself to believe that she would visit him during his month's stay in the hospital. By the time of his release, the private would be amply supported by some friends of the Fourteenth Air Force plus a few of the enlisted personnel of the United States Navy. The American private was not unduly worried about his future stay in Shanghai, the opulent "Paris of the Far East."

CHAPTER TWENTY-FIVE

It had been over three weeks since Private Goerig had last seen a khaki uniform representing another member of the Fourteenth Air Force. Despite his high manner of living and the fast-rising inflation in currency, he still had about half of the original bundles of Chinese bank notes remaining in his barracks bag. However, the inflation was getting ridiculous. In order to go out on the town for a night, a person had to carry several packages of CNC (Chinese National Currency). When you wanted to dance, somebody had to remain at the table and stand guard over the stacks of money so no petty thief would make off with it. However, George still managed to have quite a ball until that unfortunate day when the Navy came to town.

Four sailors dressed in "whites" were enjoying their first shore leave in Shanghai and helping to keep the bartender quite active. Several naval officers, with an abundance of gold braid on the sleeves of their blue uniforms, were sitting at a table in the lounge entertaining two reserved-looking ladies.

Goerig sidled up to the bar, and as he sat down, he ordered his usual, a double Scotch and soda. As his friend placed the drink down on the bar, he calmly announced, "That will be two dollars, sir."

"Two dollars!" the private hollered. "Are you nuts or something? I can get a whole bottle down on the street for two dollars!"

"I don't doubt that at all, sir, but you cannot drink it here in our establishment," he firmly answered.

George angrily turned to the sailor sitting next to him. "Well, you guys sure screwed it up for everybody. Just because you can't spend your dough for booze on your ship doesn't mean you have to throw it around like it was New Year's Eve here in Shanghai every night."

The young sailor smiled and merely nodded his head. "You're right, soldier, but what the hell else can we do? We still have to pay the price they ask for." He hesitated. "How about one on me?"

Goerig started to politely refuse when a sudden commotion drew his attention towards the middle of the room. A drunken seaman was attempting to climb up on an empty chair. He had a bottle in one hand and a fistful of Chinese currency in the other. The normal conversation had quickly become subdued when the inebriated center of attraction loudly bellowed, "Where are the girls? I got the money and I want to fuck."

Complete silence engulfed the entire room. Finally one-red faced captain rose from his seat. He promptly walked over, grabbed the man off of the chair, and quickly steered him over to two approaching shore patrolmen, who he briskly ordered, "See that this man is thrown in the brig. When I return to the ship, I want to attend to him personally."

George's sailor friend gulped down his drink and quickly whispered to his companions, "Let's get the hell out of here. This ain't no place for us."

The others nodded in agreement and shortly the private was sitting by himself. He called the bartender, Donald, to come over so he could talk with him.

"Yes sir," the man replied as he stood in front of the private. "What can I do for you?"

George leaned over and politely inquired, "Is it true the hotel management is getting a stateside orchestra in to play up on the fourteenth floor? I understand that they have completely renovated the room and are going to have a grand opening tonight for dinner and dancing. Am I right?"

"You are right, George my boy, I have been up there and it is really something. They are bringing in a group of ex-GIs from the Philippines who have been playing together quite a while. It should be a good night. We have set aside a number of reservations for several American officers who will be coming into Shanghai."

The private stared at him intently. "What's my chances of getting a table for four?"

The bartender hesitated as it became apparent he was enjoying some type of suspense he had unwittingly created. He picked up a glass and began slowly wiping it.

"All tables have been reserved," he curtly answered.

Goerig's face took on a dejected expression as he slowly stirred the ice in his drink. Finally, with a feigned look of pity, Donald continued, "But, what if I told you that four of those reservations are in your name?"

George's eyes lit up. "Why you old son of a gun, are you kidding?"

"I no kid," he laughed. "Just check out your table at the maitre d's stand as you go in."

"Have a drink on me and put it on the house tab. I won't forget you for this," the private solemnly swore.

The bartender paused and then seriously began, "George, you have been very generous to me and to all the help around here. We all appreciate it. Anything that any of us can do for you, we'll do it, if we can." He added, "I'll have that drink on you later on." He chuckled at the little trick he had played on his best customer.

George went to the phone to call Boris and inform him of the good news as well as to find out if they would be his guests for the evening. He was also anxiously hoping that Maria would join them. He had not taken Irene's advice that after the unfortunate incident, he should perhaps start going out with other girls. She had added that she had one definite girl in mind, and that certain girl would soon make him forget all about Maria. Her name was Tania and she was patiently looking forward to meeting the American. Goerig had dismissed the idea, not being able to foresee that in the near future that beautiful little white Russian doll was going to play an important role in the private's life while in Shanghai.

He was finally able to reach his good Russian friend at the latter's apartment. Fortunately, Maria was visiting with them. George explained about the new opening at the hotel and asked if they would be his guests. He then hesitated but said at last, "Please let me talk to Maria."

After a short pause, his reluctant Miss Shanghai softly answered. "Hello, George, how are you?"

He replied, "I am fine. But I didn't know you cared about my health anymore. What gives?"

Maria hesitated and Goerig found himself starting to become perturbed.

In a very somber tone, she answered, "I just found out what really happened the other night at Chi Chi's. They told you me you would probably have been killed if it wasn't for your American friends. I felt I was to blame for everything that has happened, and I decided I shouldn't see you again. I didn't want anything else to happen to you."

George tried to explain. "Look, I like you very much. We've had a wonderful time together and enjoy each other's company. Your ex-boyfriend is in the hospital with a broken neck. He asked for it. The doctor has him in traction. He says the man will be laid up for at least a couple of months. I'm sorry for what happened, but it was either him or me, and I'm allergic to hospitals. We won't be bothered again."

Then, to ease what he thought was a tense situation, he added jokingly, "Also, the Navy has landed and everything is under control."

It was good to hear her melodious laugh again. He continued, "Tonight, they have a special opening of the newly renovated night club on the fourteenth floor of the Parke Hotel. A sharp new orchestra made up of ex-GIs are going to be playing. I was lucky enough to get reservations for four. Boris, Irene, you, and myself. Maria, I am really counting on you being there. Now, please, how about it? Do I have to get down on my knees? I'll do it here in front of all these people in the lobby, if you want me to."

"No, no!" she yelled over the phone. "Don't you dare, George, I will go with you, I promise."

"Okay, it's a date. Pick you up at eight. It's formal, so wear your best." He laughed. "Because I'll be wearing mine. I hope you don't get tired of tan khakis. On me, I think they are becoming."

Maria laughed again as she seemed to relax.

"Alright, at eight o'clock. I will be waiting for you." She hung up.

George gave a whoop of joy as he emerged from the phone booth and headed for the elevators. Johnnie came running over. "Everything okay, Mister Goerig?"

"Great, just great," was the answer. "Get me a bottle of Scotch," be said, then hesitated. "No, make that three and with plenty of soda and ice. About eighty thirty, I want a large tray of the fanciest hors d'oeuvres you have brought up to my room."

The private paused again and then added, "Oh yes, a couple dozen red roses placed in vases around the suite. You can do that any time before eight thirty, but bring the Scotch up now."

George impatiently waited for one of the elevators to reach the main floor. The doors opened and a couple of shore patrol came out dragging a drunken sailor in tow. He squeezed past them and pushed the sixth-floor button. After leaving the elevator, Goerig walked over to his room. The door was ajar as he reached for the knob. Upon entering, he quickly became aware of a dark-haired maid bending over and straightening the covers on his bed. Her back was to him as he noticed approvingly that her very short skirt was not quite long enough to cover the bare expanse above the top of her sheer silk stockings. The shapely legs looked inviting. He forgot about the Scotch, temporarily.

The doll glanced up and turned around as she heard George enter.

"Oui, monsieur, can I help you?" she sweetly asked.

The private silently thought to himself, "Oh baby, can you ever."

Her face had a pert, saucy look to it and a pair of brown eyes with long lashes gazed innocently at George. The private appraisingly stared at two firm breasts straining at the square-cut top of her black uniform. The whiteness of her bare shoulders in contrast to the dress and the slight cleavage, which indicated a warm valley below, drew him to her. Purposely, he kicked the door shut with the back of his foot. Goerig then walked over and impulsively put his arms around the girl, cautiously pinning her arms to her sides.

"Baby, you certainly can, beginning now."

He bent his head down and gently placed his lips over her crimson red mouth. She momentarily struggled and then suddenly relaxed as George released her arms. She warmly placed them around his neck. He could feel every portion of her warm body as she pressed against his. His desire made him bolder as he gently picked up the little French maiden and tenderly laid her down on the yielding contours of the soft bed.

Goerig walked back and locked the door. As he laid down beside her, she turned her head, smiled, and said. "I have been waiting for you."

The would-be lover immediately sat up. "You have been waiting for me?" he exclaimed. "But you never saw me before."

Her twinkling eyes widened, and her inviting lips opened slightly.

"Oh yes, I have seen you many times, but you are always in a hurry, or with somebody. You just never noticed me." She pouted. "I finally talked to Johnnie. He told me to stop waiting around and to come to your room. So, here I am."

George's mouth fell open at the candor and frankness of the innocent-looking face patiently waiting for some reaction.

The American did not disappoint her. "Sit up," he ordered.

She sat up. He reached behind her back and pulled the zipper down till it stopped. The girl sat motionless, waiting. He then parted the back of the uniform and slowly drew it down over two pert and fully rounded breasts. She wore no brassiere. As he bent to kiss the rising nipples, which were becoming tantalizingly rigid, she put her hand over his lips. George thought, "Oh no, not again."

The little maid whispered. "Let us do it right. We shall both undress and get into the bed together. Alright?"

The astounded private quickly rolled over the edge of the bed and hastily removed his shoes and clothes. As he turned back, the French beauty doffed her uniform and stockings. She then raised her hips off the bed in order to slip a white pair of lace panties down over them. As she bent over, the tips of her firm, naked breasts brushed against her bare legs.

Divested of all her clothing, the girl quickly jumped up and pulled back the covers on the bed. Sliding between the satin sheets, she hungrily reached out her arms toward George. Needing no further encouragement, he moved in beside the waiting doll and took her in his arms. Tenderly, Goerig drew her to him till he could feel every sensitive portion of her eager, enticing body. Then suddenly he drew back and stupidly asked, "Are you really French?"

"Does it really matter?" came the whispered reply.

The stinging spray of cold water was invigorating as Goerig washed the remaining lather off his body. He was disappointed when Marie had smilingly rejected his suggestion that they take a shower together. She had been afraid that perhaps one of the hotel employees might come looking for her.

He turned off the faucet, grabbed one of the large Turkish towels, and walked into the living room. His bed had been neatly made over and a small note was on the pillow. It read simply, "My name is Marie, not Maria, in case you are still interested. Thank you for the glorious time."

George smiled to himself. "Yeah, thanks, Johnnie. I needed that."

Picking up the unopened bottle of Scotch, he pulled out the cork and poured a very stiff shot into a tall glass. The seltzer bottle furnished the additional ingredient as he dropped a handful of ice in after the soda. Raising his glass, he mockingly looked at himself in the mirror. "Here's cheers and I hope a pleasant evening." If he knew who he was going to face that night, he probably would have settled for a straight ginger ale.

Goerig looked at his watch. It was six thirty. Plenty of time, he thought. Perhaps another one for the road? He hesitated then said to himself, "Nope, it's going to be a long evening and I'd better play it cool."

His silent monologue was starting to get the best of him. However, he figured that as long as he didn't talk too loud to himself, nobody would notice.

CHAPTER TWENTY-SIX

As George passed through the hotel lobby, he noticed several couples in formal attire, chatting in subdued conversations. He silently mused, "I'm sure glad I've got my formal on. I wonder what the girls are going to wear."

The trip to Boris's apartment was uneventful as the private had practically memorized the location of the buildings along the way. He didn't realize it then, but it was going to be quite a factor on one night in the near future. In fact, it saved his life.

As Goerig walked into Boris's small apartment, he was met by the his strikingly beautiful blonde wife. She had her hair done up in a bun behind her head. The long evening gown she wore sparkled with tiny sequins. George suddenly became embarrassed by the fact that he had never complimented Irene on her outstanding figure. His feelings toward Boris's wife had been more like a brother-sister relation and his sexual attraction about her had been nil even if he had been struck by her beauty. Tonight was different, however. The low-cut gown she wore partially revealed two enticing mounds of a bosom that must have kept Boris busy on the cold nights living in the French Concession.

George reluctantly averted his gaze as he turned to the genial host, who was patiently waiting with two drinks in his hands.

"'Boris, you are married to one of the greatest beauties I have ever had the pleasure to cast my eyes upon."

They clicked their high balls together.

"Swebien." Goerig recalled the Chinese phrase and added, "as much as you like." He then proudly and stupidly explained. "Chinese, of course, you know."

"Yes, Georges we know very well," Boris politely replied. "We have lived in China all of our lives." He laughed. "Shall I call a cab?"

By the time they had finished their drinks, the cab was waiting for them as they came out on the sidewalk. When they arrived at Maria's apartment, she was watching from the window; she waved and indicated that she would be right down. George held the cab door open, and as the girl climbed in, he couldn't help but notice the aroma of an exotic perfume that wafted over him.

"You certainly smell nice, tonight," he inadvertently mentioned.

The four of them rode in the back seat, with Irene perched on her husband's lap and with George casually draping his arm over Maria's warm shoulder. As they arrived at their destination, a tall, uniformed doorman opened the cab door in front of the Parke Hotel. They ducked their heads as they left the coke-burning vehicle. Walking up the steps, they passed through the revolving doors. Boris and George checked Irene and Maria's coats as the girls left to perform their usual last-minute rituals in the powder room.

George approached the maitre d' at his station by the entrance to the supper club. He was busily scanning the names on his select list of evening patrons who would be celebrating the grand reopening. George moved forward and drew the man's attention by gently tapping him on the shoulder. The latter locked up and haughtily asked, "Name, please?"

"Private George Goerig and party, sir."

A startled expression caused the man's eyebrows to raise as he glanced back at his list. Finally, he unclasped the sacred rope that barred the portal to his personal domain.

The private naturally thought they would be given a table on the outer limits of the club. As they continued to weave past the crowded tables, their host finally stopped at one adjacent to the dance floor. He graciously pulled back one of the chairs as Maria moved in and sat down. He then meticulously drew back a chair across the table and waited for Irene to be seated. As he removed the "reserved" card, he briskly announced, "A waiter will be here shortly."

Boris looked around the room and, unable to conceal his surprise at their good fortune, whispered aside to his American host for the evening, "Who do you know so well as to be able to get the best table in the room?"

Goerig lightly brushed his fingertips up and down the front of his khaki shirt in a feigned manner and proclaimed to all, "Oh, I've got my friends."

His mind recalled three at the time: Johnnie, the bellhop, Donald, the bartender, and last but not least, Ashley the desk clerk.

The animated hum of conversation and the tinkling of the ice in the glasses provided a melodious background to George's ears. The dark glow of hidden lights on the walls of the room gave the warm feeling of a romantic setting. He glanced at Maria. "Like it?" he asked hopefully.

She grasped his hand and squeezed it for a moment. "Love it" was the answer.

The orchestra was beginning to get ready by individually tuning up their instruments. Goerig was particularly interested in a tall negro sitting by the drums while another agile-fingered man was testing the keyboard on the piano. He thought to himself, "Boy, this is going to be good."

The leader walked over in front of the group as the band became quiet. He softly tapped his foot in rhythm and abruptly swung his baton. The beautiful, familiar strains of "Night and Day" came over the suddenly hushed audience. George clasped Maria's hand and rose from his chair. "Come on, darling, that's my song. Let's dance."

She eagerly got up and the two stepped out on the floor. The girl nestled herself in his arms as he promptly took advantage of the small dance area. They realized that shortly it would become too crowded to enjoy dancing to the music. After a few minutes, George suggested that they sit down and watch the others struggling among themselves. The couple was soon engrossed in an intimate discussion of past happenings since they had been apart. After several rounds of drinks, however, the private noticed that his girl was becoming uneasy and nervous. She would occasionally glance over towards a table to the side and then turn back. Her cheeks were beginning to get flushed. Finally, Maria leaned over and in a puzzled manner, asked, "Is it proper for your officers to continually stare at someone they don't know?"

She silently nodded her head to the left. George followed her gaze to a table of five American Air Force officers, who seemed to be enjoying the evening's festivities. His mouth fell open as he moaned, "Oh no, dear God, there is my boss. It looks like the honeymoon is over."

Complacently sitting at the nearby table was General Stone, who had replaced General Chenault, with four attentive colonels. One especially, who had caught the private's eye, was wearing the engineer's castle insignia on his collar. The man seemed intently interested in the enlisted soldier holding hands with a very beautiful girl.

Maria looked at her date. "What do you mean by 'your boss'?"

Rising from his chair, he hastily answered. "I'll tell you about it later." He then paused. "If I ever get the chance."

George was hoping the tipsy feeling buzzing in his head would go away as he approached the general's table. The engineering officer seemed to be patiently waiting as the curious group of men became strangely silent.

"Colonel Freeburn, Private Goerig reporting for duty, sir."

The embarrassed enlisted man saluted in the best manner he could recall. It had been a long time. The officer leaned back in his chair and seemed to be pleasantly enjoying their first confrontation.

"Private Goerig," he slowly began, "if I'm not mistaken, I believe you are listed as absent without leave. That means in the army vernacular, you are AWOL. Now, may I kindly ask what the hell you are doing here?"

George hastily reached in his back pocket for his wallet. After opening it up, he withdrew a leather-stained piece of paper. Unfolding it and handing it to the colonel, he dutifully explained, "Sir, Captain Lewis gave me these orders when I was in Laifeng. At the time, I was under the impression I was supposed to go to Sian. But as you can see, I believe they were changed for me to go to Shanghai. I think they are in order, sir."

The short explanation was being intently listened to by the other officers at the table. They were all waiting for the private's superior to answer. The latter briefly scanned the papers in his hand and then returned them.

"Well, they seem to be alright. The only thing that puzzles me is why the hell didn't Captain Lewis turn in a duplicate copy to headquarters before he left for New York. As far as the records are concerned, you are still AWOL."

The colonel didn't seem to be very perturbed about Goerig's apparent nervousness. He abruptly changed the topic of conversation. Looking past the enlisted man's shoulder, he naively inquired, "Is that beautiful girl with you tonight?"

George glanced back at a worried-looking Maria. "Yes sir" was the answer.

Freeburn, without hesitation, bluntly asked, "Mind if I join you?"

"No sir." Goerig felt a quick sense of relief come over him. He added, "I would like it, sir."

The officer rose from his seat and courteously asked to be excused by the general. At that time another Colonel eagerly tugged at his companion's coat. "How about me, Larry?"

Freeburn quizzically turned. "Okay, George, if we make it for two?"

"Fine sir, I believe we can find room."

As the three started to leave, General Stone smiled and, turning to his attentive aides, remarked, "Well, that didn't take very long for a reprimand, did it?"

His subordinates obediently laughed and then enviously watched as their two compatriots started over to the other table. Additional chairs were brought in by the harassed waiter. Goerig introduced the colonel to his guests. Freeburn stared at the embarrassed Maria and finally said, "George, your girlfriend is beautiful."

"That is what I also think, sir" was the reply.

The evening was a success even though Boris and his American friend sat by themselves a good portion of the time as the two officers monopolized their dates. Finally, George looked over to Boris.

"I hope you don't mind my bringing them over, do you?"

"No, George. In fact, this gives me a chance to talk to you about that certain little favor I thought you might be able to do for me sometime."

"Go ahead, I'm listening." The private reached for his glass and took a drink.

Boris began, "You know I am a food broker. As you have told me, your Fourteenth Air Force is going to move into Shanghai. I would like the opportunity to supply them with any food products they will need, if it is possible. What do you think?"

"Hell yes" was the quick answer. "If I'm not mistaken, I believe that short guy dancing with your wife is the fellow to talk to. From his conversation tonight, I think he is the quartermaster officer in charge of supplies, and that will be right down your alley."

The Russian looked surprised. "What do you mean by 'down my alley'?"

George had to laugh at his friend's question. "Boris, don't worry. It is merely a colloquialism. It means that your business could be a big help to him."

The two officers with the girls were returning to the table.

It was just the beginning of an evening during which George and Boris were going to spend the majority of the time watching their eager guests monopolize the attention of Irene and Maria. Goerig did manage to have the last dance with his date as the dying strains of "Til We Meet Again" were supposed to indicate the end of the social activities for the night. However, his expectations were not shared by Colonel Freeburn.

In a commanding voice, he ordered, "Alright, let's the six of us go out on the town and see what we can find. George, you and Boris should know of a few night spots that are open late. I'm just beginning to have a good time. How about it? Okay?"

He then gave Maria a playful hug. "How about it, dear? Wouldn't you like it?"

"Certainly," she condescendingly answered. "Whatever George wants to do."

The latter felt momentarily flattered at her sudden concern for his neglected feelings. Resigned to the fact that their quiet evening had been changed into a prospective group revelry, Goerig nodded his head. Rising from his chair, he took Maria by the hand and started the exodus towards the door. Both colonels had hurriedly excused themselves from General Stone and were belatedly following.

The supposedly congenial group entered a taxicab in front of the hotel and proceeded to make a tour of several all-night dance spots. George was getting tired, but Maria was doing well in her role as a charming hostess to the out-of-town guests.

Boris was excitedly making plans with Colonel Neupert in regard to furnishing the Fourteenth with the necessary food stables upon their arrival in Shanghai. The short officer at the same time was continually staring at the beautiful Irene. It was a good set up.

At about five o'clock in the morning, when the party had finally broken up, Goerig found himself saying good night to his colonel in the lobby of the hotel.

"It has been an enjoyable evening, sir," he said, lying. "I hope you had a good time."

"George, it has been a tremendous evening, and I want to thank you very much. Maria is a wonderful girl. By the way, we are leaving at eight o'clock this morning. I want to meet you here at that time." He paused and then continued. "I did intend to take you back to Chungking with me. However, I am going to let you stay in Shanghai on two conditions."

The private sensed a feeling of relief. "What are they, sir?"

The officer lowered his voice as though he was going to ask a very confidential favor. "The general and I will be back in Shanghai shortly to set up a permanent base here. I want you to fix the both of us up with an apartment and find two girls as pretty and charming as Maria for future dates. Is it a deal?"

The seriousness of his facial expression belied the joyful reaction George felt.

He quickly and confidently answered, "Consider it done, sir. I'll fix you up with nothing but the best."

The colonel continued as he looked at his watch. "Meet me here in the lobby at eight o'clock sharp. Don't forget. You won't get much sleep. You can catch up later."

The two shook hands and Goerig headed for his room.

It seemed as though he had just laid his head on the pillow when a call came from the desk.

"Time to get up, sir. It is seven thirty."

Rushing into the bathroom, George washed his face and shaved. Throwing some talcum powder under his arms, Goerig hastily dressed and was down in the lobby again, slightly before eight. Colonel Freeburn was waiting. He immediately got down to business.

"George, there will be an advance party arriving in the next few days. I want you to take care of them. We'll be taking over a small airport just south of Shanghai. I have a lot of work lined out for you to do. The reports on the job you did in Laifeng have been most satisfactory, and I am sure you are capable of handling any problems that may come up here."

Then as an afterthought he reached in his coat pocket and drew out a pair of stripes. "You can pin these on anytime, Corporal Goerig, when you get the time. You won't get rich, but at least it is something we can do in appreciation for your past efforts." Hesitatingly, he added, "Oh, by the way, you are in line for the Bronze Star. Captain Lewis submitted a request for the award. You deserve it."

George looked up at his superior guiltily and then confessed, "I have to admit I wrote out the recommendation for the medal, sir. Captain Lewis just signed it."

The private patiently waited for a well-deserved reprimand. Instead, the colonel put his hand assumingly on Goerig's shoulder. He laughed. "I figured you wrote it. The commendation was too flowery and complimentary for Captain Lewis. He normally is very abrupt in his correspondence. It makes no difference since you earned it. That is what counts."

As Freeburn turned to leave, he paused. "We'll be having some equipment moving in here shortly. You are going to be a busy lad. One of the jeeps will be for you. Latch on to it and don't let anyone, including officers, try and take it away from you. It will be yours as long as you are in Shanghai."

Goerig smartly saluted as the officer joined two other colonels who were patiently waiting for him in the foyer. A feeling of exhilaration surged through his body as he rushed over to the phone to call Boris and relate the good news. After a few rings, Irene answered. Her husband was still in bed, but she would awaken him. In the background, the American could hear her urgently trying to rouse her spouse. Finally, a sleepy voice was on the other end.

"What are you calling for so early in the morning?"

"Boris, I've got it made!" was the excited reply.

Sleepily, he asked, "What do you mean, 'you have it made'?"

George slowly explained what the colonel had told him that morning. Receiving no immediate response, he continued, "How did you and Colonel Neupert make out on the food deal?"

Suddenly the Russian became wide awake. "Oh, fine, just fine. I am to meet with a certain major who will acquaint me with the necessary items that will be required. Thank you, George." Then he added, "By the way, how about you coming out tonight for dinner? Maria will be here, and we can discuss our mutual good luck."

"Boris, I'd love to."

Naturally, Goerig was anxious to learn of his past date's reactions to his very attentive superior.

"I'll be there at six o'clock. Okay?"

"Very well. Six it is."

"Thanks, Boris. Now go back to sleep. You need it. Sorry for waking you up."

Walking over to a spacious sofa, George sat down to contemplate his change of status as an elevated corporal in the services of the Fourteenth

Air Force. Soberly, he gazed around at the surrounding, now that he knew he was going to have to move out shortly. It had been a lot of fun, and he knew he was going to miss it. Unobtrusively, the bell captain, Johnnie, came over with a worried expression on his face. He asked, "Everything all right, Mister Goerig?"

"Fine, just fine" was the reply. "Except that I'm going to have to move out within the week. My outfit is coming in and taking over that small airport south of town. It means back to work for me."

Disappointedly, the boy replied, "We will all be sorry to see you leave us, sir. You certainly have livened things up around here. I hope you won't forget us."

George rose from his chair and grasped Johnnie's hand. "I won't, boy. Now would you please send up a couple of Bloody Marys? I think I may go back to bed for a while and catch up on some needed sleep."

"Yes, sir. Coming right up."

Goerig crossed the lobby and went on to the elevators. After all, there was still an important evening to look forward to.

═

It was a happy group as both Boris and Maria excitedly recalled the events of the previous night. The girl sincerely told George how much she was sorry about the situation where his superior had monopolized most of the dances. Meanwhile, Boris was unnecessarily apologizing to his wife about the preoccupied discussions he had had with the quartermaster officer. It seemed that the young Russian had the possible food contract under control. To nobody's surprise, Maria admitted that, following a request for a date in the future from Colonel Freeburn, she had accepted. Hesitatingly, she looked the corporal.

"Is that all right, George?"

The latter shrugged his shoulders as though to indicate there wasn't much he could do about it. "Well, certainly."

Not to be outdone, however, he looked over at Irene and politely asked, "How about that Tania girl, you mentioned? Is she still available?

It looks like I am going to have to find a new female friend here in Shanghai."

Irene curiously glanced over at her girlfriend's startled expression. Looking back at the American, she surprised him by remarking, "Well, I am sure Tania would love it. I know Maria would not mind. The both of them are very good friends. Tania was also a contestant in the Miss Shanghai contest last year."

Boris suddenly entered the conversation. "Why no, Tania is a very beautiful girl, isn't she, Maria? We know you would not mind, would you?"

A quickly subdued girl with pouting lips murmured as she started to sip her drink, "At least you could have waited until I had left. "

Leaning over, George tenderly kissed her on the cheek. "It looks like we both might be very happy with a change. As long as we keep it all in the family."

With this, the foursome broke out laughing. The tenseness that had suddenly come over them quickly vanished. Meanwhile, Goerig was definitely looking forward to his prospective meeting with the popular and intriguing Tania.

The next few days were hectic as Corporal Goerig found himself busy with the organization and indirect supervision of a couple of hundred Chinese coolies. His first primary project was to clean up and renovate the barracks recently vacated by the Japanese army personnel. A slightly used jeep had been placed at his disposal by a confused lieutenant who seemed puzzled at the orders he had been given. The man had been instructed that one Corporal Goerig was to have complete freedom in carrying out his assignments. The enlisted man was to be responsible only to a Major Forrest.

At his first opportunity, George moved in to a single large room in his new quarters. He had sadly transferred his belongings out of the Parke Hotel. Fortunately, however, they included a hastily purchased case of Black and White Scotch, "strictly for medicinal purposes." While Johnnie put Goerig's barracks bag in the back of the jeep, he turned wistfully to his American friend.

"Well, sir, it has been a real pleasure serving you. I hope you will find the time to stop back. Please do not forget where we are. Come see us when you have free time."

George assured the bell hop captain that he would. As he climbed in the jeep, he turned and handed the boy a large manila envelope. "Here, Johnnie, is a small token of my appreciation. Don't spend it all in one place." Looking up at the impressive facade of his former home, he added, "I'm going to miss it here. Well, goodbye and good luck."

The corporal cautiously moved his newly acquired vehicle out into the bustling traffic and silently wondered if his Shanghai honeymoon was finally over. Fortunately, he was just moving out of one local phase into another. He had grown fond of Shanghai, but he was sincerely looking forward to the new challenge offered to him by Colonel Freeburn.

═

After a very active month following the Fourteenth's move into the metropolitan area, Goerig slowly began to realize he had unwittingly acquired the function of being the social chairman for quite a few of the officers and enlisted men. His nodding acquaintance with some of the white Russian girls beside Maria and Irene had naturally become obvious to the Air Force engineering personnel. It wasn't long before the suddenly popular corporal was being besieged by requests for introductions to the available single girls he casually knew in the French and International Concessions.

Goerig was hopeful, to a certain extent, that the engineers he introduced to the various members of the opposite sex he had met would behave themselves so he wouldn't have to apologize to any of the Russian parents for their daughters getting pregnant. All in all, the majority of the white Russian girls had high moral values. He had found out the hard way.

Regarding the types that dominated the bar at Chi Chi's, that selection of promiscuous women offered a variety of sex that came in all colors and sizes with an assortment of special tricks to sate the long-dormant sexual appetite of any GI. Hence, there was something for everybody. It was not called the "Paris of the East" in vain.

Another feature attraction that most of the engineers, including Goerig, thought of as a "must" was the obtaining of available Japanese souvenirs. The first real opportunity presented itself when George received orders to take a work gang over to the former Japanese professors' apartments, adjacent to Shanghai University.

Having been unceremoniously evicted from the deluxe living quarters furnished to the teachers, these groups were forced to leave behind most of their possessions. The prized belongings, which Goerig found, mostly consisted of an assortment of beautiful large geisha dolls dressed in their native, ancient costumes and encased in glass show cases. He immediately laid claim to several of these and had them properly packaged and shipped back home.

Expensive cameras of all types and movie projectors were prime targets. Actually, it was like going on a giant scavenger hunt with very valuable free rewards for the offering. However, the most prized souvenir of the war unfortunately eluded the corporal during an occurrence that could have possibly proved fatal to him. The event was shortcoming.

The largest hospital in the city was named after the father of the Chinese Nationalist Party, Sun Yat-sen. It was a six-story concrete building that the Japanese had taken over and converted into a military hospital. This imposing edifice had been used solely to provide medical facilities for the wounded war casualties resulting from the Japanese hostilities.

Goerig's new assignment included the cleanup of the unsanitary, deplorable conditions existing at the badly deteriorated hospital and make it presentable for occupation by the Chinese military forces. The corporal silently questioned how such a project had been included the Air Corps Engineers' Manual of Operations. However, he was happy and satisfied about the responsibility placed upon him for a massive renovation.

During his first day at the medical facility, George was astounded and could hardly believe his eyes at the abominable situation and the lack of normal customary action to remedy the same. Sewer downspouts had broken and human excrement was piled up around the base of the shattered pipes. The obnoxious stench was overpowering, and the sickening air was suffocating. It was a cleanup job the Chinese coolies had to do.

Inside the hospital, the problems were of a different nature. Room after room in the storage area was filled with bundles of roots, herbs, and miscellaneous so-called cure alls. Rats the size of cats ran all over the closeted sections and were found nesting among the roots and the herbs.

It was impossible to conceive such a deplorable situation in a so-called modern hospital. To George, it seemed a throwback to ancient times. All the corporal could perceive was that the foreseeable loss of the war had created a sense of hopelessness and despair among the medical personnel. They probably didn't give a damn.

Goerig's first official meeting with a ranking Japanese medical officer was with a Major Yamashita. He was very courteous and bowed several times at their first introduction. The corporal quickly informed the officer that he was not accustomed to such formal attention and politely told him to forget it.

When their initial conversation began, George was amazed at the major's perfect English. It seemed that he was a graduate of Columbia University in New York City and had spent a good deal of time in the United States prior to the war. His complacent attitude was disarming as he talked about his future plans to teach in one of the colleges back in the States. Surprisingly, the confident officer also mentioned the fact that he was definitely going to finish his post-graduate course in medical research at Columbia.

"What makes you think you will be welcome or even be allowed to return to the United States after your complicity before and during the war?" George asked. "I'll bet you did a little spying for your own country when you were going to school at Columbia."

The Major laughed. "Now, Mister Goerig, you Americans forget things very fast. Wait and you will see the Japanese people rise again and soon become one of the leading industrial nations in the world despite the devastation and destruction wrought on our cities and factories." Confidently and smugly, he continued, "Look at Germany in World War I. Germany was crushed and yet a few years later it managed to produce the greatest war machine the world had ever known. That was done under the very noses of Great Britain, France, and your own country. Your people ignored the rise of Hitler and the military power of the Japanese. It took a stupid surprise attack on Pearl Harbor to shake you out of your sleep. I believe the next time your people will be more cautious. Mister Goerig, there is nothing you can do to stop the rise of our industrial might." He hesitated. "In fact, your country will be the biggest market for our future exports. Please wait and you will see."

The magnitude and impact of his brief dissertation left the American speechless. What he had said could all be very true. George preferred to change the subject. The two were sitting on the ledge of the roof overlooking the sprawling metropolis below them. As the conversation waned, Major Yamashita reached down into his medical bag at his side. Opening it up, he withdrew a pair of binoculars. He handed them to George, and meanwhile acting the part of a courteous host—which he was—he suggested, "Please take these, Mister Goerig, and I will attempt to show you the main points of interest in the great city of Shanghai."

After unnecessarily instructing George in the simple matter of adjusting the powerful field glasses, the officer, with an outstretched arm, began pointing out the various sections of the fabulous city. Of primary interest to George was a fairly large area in the middle of Shanghai encircled by a massive crumbling brick wall. Upon inquiring about this unique structure, he received an interesting answer.

"That is the old Chinese city. It was surrounded by a brick-faced wall over three miles in circumference. It was partially pulled down sometime during the years of 1912 or 1913. It is a characteristically old Chinese town of narrow paved streets with many small shops and stores."

After pointing out several other famous landmarks of the town and unintentionally confusing the corporal with the Chinese names the latter was having a hard time digesting, the officer finished his talk with, "Is there anything else I might interest you in?"

Goerig immediately took the opportunity to broach a subject that had constantly been in the back of his mind.

"Major, I am interested in obtaining a couple of samurai swords for souvenirs. Is it possible you might be able to locate them for me here in the hospital?"

The doctor hesitated and finally nodded his head.

"Why yes, I believe that could be arranged."

Having achieved that goal, George thought he might as well go a little farther and ask for the ultimate in souvenirs.

"How about a general's sword? I figure you must have at least one of your highest-ranking officers as a patient here in the hospital. Do you actually believe that he would rather turn his most treasured possession over to an American rather than a Chinese?"

The reply was immediate and very curt. "There are no generals here."

Goerig was momentarily taken aback by the brusque response. He decided it would be useless to push the subject and figured he might as well be content with what he could get. The major excused himself, stating he would be back shortly. After a half hour or so, the man returned with the two cherished swords under his arm. Presenting them to the American, he explained, "The brown scabbard belonged to a major in the Army, while this black one was owned by a captain in the Navy."

"Thank you. I appreciate this," George answered with gratitude.

As he accepted the prized souvenirs, he thought how impressive they would be to his friends back in the States. He didn't believe Helen would appreciate them. Too much. However, he figured that the geisha dolls would make her happy.

The unexpected incident occurred a few days later as the corporal parked his jeep in front of the hospital and was walking over to the steps of the main entrance.

A large contingent of Chinese soldiers was standing at attention in front of several commandeered military cars. Goerig looked up as a party of Japanese emerged out of the doors of the medical facility. An unusually husky but pale-looking officer, his military coat draped over his shoulders, was being supported by two aides. As the man slowly walked down the steps, George immediately recognized the general's insignia on his uniform. He reflected back to his recent conversation with the Japanese major and angrily mumbled to himself. "Why that rotten bastard. He lied to me."

But, what the hell, the Nips had been lying for years before Pearl Harbor. So what else was new?

Despite the formidable-looking escort, the corporal boldly approached the faltering general. He was about to demand the samurai sword that hung loosely at his side. The useless merely demonstrative weapon represented the last vestige remaining of the officer's military career. However, as George was about to demand the release of the prized possession, he became acutely aware of the glaring, menacing eyes of the military escort.

Unconsciously, he recalled the sagacious saying that entered his mind: "Sometimes discretion is the better part of valor." Realizing that any slight provocation on his part could be cause for a fatal attack on his own precious life, Goerig wisely moved back, turned, and headed for his jeep.

Racing toward his new quarters at the airfield, the corporal figured a few reinforcements and a conspicuous forty-five side arm would amply provide him with the sufficient false courage he needed to face the precarious situation. At the same time, he was hoping the general would still be at the hospital when he returned.

Goerig impatiently pulled up in front of his barracks. Climbing out, he hollered over to three non-coms idly standing by the doorway.

"Want a quick ride into town? I might need some help."

The question seemed more like an order than a request due to the urgency in Goerig's voice. Without any ado, the three men jumped into the waiting vehicle. Meanwhile, George had gone into his room, grabbed his holstered forty-five, and was buckling the belt as he emerged from the building. Getting in behind the wheel of the jeep, he quickly spun it around and headed back into town. The presence of the three husky aviation engineers gave him a renewed confidence that bolstered his courage for the job ahead.

Despite breaking all posted speed limits and going through several stop signs, the four arrived a little too late. The blue exhaust from the bail pipes of the receding cars had left a faint haze where they had disappeared.

"Dammit!" Goerig disappointedly yelled as his three puzzled passengers looked askance at him. It was then that the corporal apologetically explained the purpose of his futile mission. The non-coms waited expectantly for his next move, and then George suddenly jumped out of the jeep and shouted over his shoulder, "Come on!" He motioned for the men to follow him up the steps to the entrance of the hospital. Walking through the main corridor past some of his gawking coolies, the corporal waved his arm towards the empty rooms.

"There are a helluva a lot more sword and souvenirs still here in those wards. I'll point out the officers' quarters, and you guys go in there and shake them down. Grab anything you want. What we don't get, the Chink bastards will."

With a loud whoop, the sergeants joyfully expressed their feelings and began converging on the various wards. After an hour of searching and selecting the choice items that appealed to their personal likes, the trio returned to the jeep loaded with their newly acquired spoils. The take included quite a number of samurai swords and Nipponese momentums. After piling the loot in the rear of the vehicle, George started it up and with spinning wheels smoking on the pavement, headed back to the airbase.

The laughing, joking, thankful engineers gave the driver a warm feeling of satisfaction as he recalled the phrase, "Giving is much more satisfying than receiving," or something like that. Either way, the quotation seemed highly appropriate to the afternoon's plundering.

═

The cleanup and renovation work at the hospital was progressing smoothly. Goerig figured they were far ahead of the proposed schedule he had given the Chinese foremen through his interpreter. In turn, he was also anxious to talk with Colonel Freeburn in regard to all the projects he had been assigned and to learn of his reaction.

Meanwhile, his superior had returned to Shanghai and was in the process of setting up a post-war debarkation center. George had been so busy and engrossed in his various jobs that he had passed up the long-awaited introduction to his new prospective girlfriend, Tania. It had been rumored that Freeburn had been wining and dining Maria. Apparently, he was more than satisfied with the young and beautiful girl. Boris and Irene were being the perfect host and hostess. The Russian played his role perfectly with the anticipated monetary results in view.

George was busy inspecting some newly renovated rooms in the hospital when he was surprised by a booming voice behind him. "What the hell are you doing now?" The question could have come from only one person. The corporal turned and laughingly inquired, "What's new, sir?"

Glancing briefly behind him, Freeburn leaned over and softly whispered in his protégé's ear, "I'll tell you what's new. Tonight, you are going to finally meet Tania and we are going out with Boris and Irene for a little party. It is Maria's birthday, and I am going to pick up the tab. Boris has you all set up. How about that, boy?"

The welcomed good news and sudden change of events left George momentarily speechless. Finally, he happily answered, "That sounds great to me, sir. When and where do we start?"

"Tonight, at seven o'clock sharp. We are to meet at Boris's apartment. Tania will be there, and I'll pick up Maria. We'll have cocktails and then we'll move out to a quaint little restaurant that Maria made reservations at. We'll have a nice, quiet dinner with all the trimmings. After that we'll wind up the night at Chi Chi's. How does that sound to you?"

George was momentarily overwhelmed by the preparations the colonel had made. "That is great, sir, just great." Then jokingly he added, "Should I wear my white tie and tails?"

Freeburn chuckled. "No, that won't be necessary. Just put on that new set of khakis I saw you picking up at the commissary yesterday."

As the man turned to go, the corporal quipped, "I'll be there with buttons and bows."

"George, if it's regulation, you can wear anything you want."

═

Goerig had resigned himself to the fact that his past affair with Maria was finished. He had no regrets, only pleasant memories of a warm and mutual friendship with a girl who had conveniently introduced him to the Shanghai night life that he really enjoyed. As he looked back upon their acquaintanceship, he realized that the idea of sexual relations between them had never entered his mind. He felt no remorse at leaving her in the capable hands of the colonel. Wasn't it Shakespeare who once said, "Good night, good night. Parting is such sweet sorrow"?

When George followed Colonel Freeburn and Maria into Boris's apartment the following night, he was not exactly prepared for gorgeous vision before him. A thought raced through his mind: "This is impossible. How could such a beautiful girl only be a runner-up? Here is a real winner."

Tania was truly beautiful. Her radiant features were exquisite and her shining dark hair provided the perfect background for the brown, captivating eyes and the provocative, sensuous lips. The dimples in her soft cheeks reacted incredibly with the welcoming smile she gave George as Irene introduced the two. George almost spoiled the first meeting with the Russian girl by stupidly saying, "Where have you been all my life?" Fortunately, he was more discreet as he more reservedly stated, "You are beautiful."

A slight perceptive blush came over her face, and she looked at Irene in an embarrassed but flattered way. As she turned back to George, she modestly regained her composure. The American melted as the soft tones of her voice came through to him.

"Are all Americans as honest as you?"

The frank response momentarily flustered her date, but George hastily replied, "No, not really. But I do want to tell you that I feel I am a very lucky boy right now."

At this inappropriate time, the colonel briskly interrupted the corporal's brief reverie with a seemingly polite order.

"Well, let's all of you sit down and relax. I'm going to mix the cocktails. Martinis or Manhattans?" he asked as he pulled out the necessary ingredients from his huge overcoat pockets.

At that time nobody was in a mood to argue with the formidable eagle on Freeburn's collar. Boris indicated the direction of the kitchen while the guests removed their coats and sat down. George made an obvious move so he could be sitting next to his sparkling and luscious new date.

Goerig's attention had been so concentrated on Tania'a fascinating features that he had surprisingly overlooked her luxurious figure. As the girl bent over to retrieve a dropped handkerchief, George immediately became aware of two partially hidden breasts. Their soft creamy roundness called forth a surge of sexual desire rising up in his body that seemed to temporarily embarrass him. Discreetly, he turned his head and groped for the tempting Manhattan that had been placed on the table.

Before he could begin a conversation, Tania turned and asked, "Well, how do you like Shanghai? I understand you have been quite busy enjoying our night life."

"It has truly been a rewarding experience for them. As for myself, I have been looking forward to meeting you for quite a while."

Her frank and disarming approach gave George a warm and contented feeling. He sensed himself comfortably relaxing as he sank back in the couch and casually draped one arm over the back of the sofa behind Tania. He took a sip of his stimulating drink and then confidently leaned over to whisper in her ear.

"I like you very much. I know we are going to have a marvelous time together tonight." Goerig paused; then anxiously asked, 'Do you like to dance?'"

Her radiant face lit up and her deep brown eyes glistened. "Dance? I love to dance. I would rather dance than eat."

Goerig's laughed. "Well, you know that is cheaper, especially with the present inflation."

The corporal's third potent cocktail had been passed to him while his new doll was still sipping on her first. Colonel Freeburn was happily performing his duties as a jovial bartender in a generous mood by amply fortifying each pitcher with extra jiggers of booze. However, he was showing no signs of intoxication. Meanwhile, George was beginning to feel a warm glow come over him. His animated conversation with Tania soon enveloped the two in an intimate world of their own as they unintentionally ignored the gaiety of the rest of the group. Before they realized it, the time had gone by too quickly, and they found themselves out in the street climbing into one of the larger cabs available in Shanghai. It happened to be a seven-passenger vehicle, which the colonel had ordered specially for the evening. As Goerig settled back in the seat, he wondered what his superior had in mind. Curiously, he asked, "Where to, boss?"

Maria, perched on her escort's lap, surprisingly responded, "I told Larry about Nicholas's restaurant out in the International Settlement. He thought it would be fine. I have called and my good friend said he is going to prepare a special table and a surprise for us."

It was very stupid that Goerig felt a little perturbed at his former doll's familiarity with the colonel's name. Before the evening was over, however, all military formalities were to be dispensed with, and Larry was a good name for a terrific person.

Nicholas greeted the jovial little group at the door of his cafe and immediately proceeded to give the same ardent welcoming reception for Tania he had previously given to Maria. Now that he had his two little babuskas under his protective wing, he proudly showed them off as he moved past the lively and appreciative customers, finally stopping at a large candle-lit table.

There were special name cards at each dinner setting. Maria had thought of everything. George was happy for her as he recalled their last unpleasant confrontation in the restaurant with her former boyfriend.

Everybody had been seated when the Colonel ordered a round of cocktails. George could soon see that the men were going to enjoy the responsibility of taking care of the major portion of the alcoholic beverages for the night. The three girls were being very gracious and polite by occasionally sipping at their drinks.

Menus were passed around the table, and Goerig was amazed at the tempting dishes they provided. He hadn't seen such a list before.

Caviar with Lemon Juice
Herring with Mustard Dill Sauce
Radishes • Minced Mushrooms
Vodka • Kvass
Shchi with Pirozhki • Borsch
Ring Mold of Sterlet • Coulibac of Salmon
Roast Partridge • Roast Turkey• Roast Duckling with Potatoes
Karavi • Guriev Kasha • Fruits • Nuts• Bastilles of Fruit

George gasped. He was familiar with most of the main courses. However, Nicholas had prepared a menu that confused him with the variety of Russian names. Pleadingly, he turned to Tania and politely asked, "Darling, could you please help me out in regard to what some of these words mean in English? I want to be sure of what I am going to enjoy for the evening."

The girl softly laughed and began to explain and describe the various Russian dishes. After a few minutes, Goerig hesitantly interrupted, "Honey, why don't you just take it from here? I trust your judgement."

The colonel, in turn, looked up from his menu with embarrassment and sighed. "I believe I'm going to have to give up also. It is too confusing, though enticing. Everything looks so good." Looking at Maria, he suggested, "I think you had better help me out also."

The two girls glanced at each other and then Tania replied, "You men are in good hands, fortunately, if I may say so. Isn't that right, Maria?"

Maria nodded her head, and within a few minutes the entire dinner selections had been made. The tuxedoed waiter, who had been dutifully standing by, bowed and left.

"You didn't forget the vodka, did you dear?" Freeburn quickly asked.

Tania (right) with the author, George Goerig, next to Irene And Boris Olienakov

"No sir," Maria courteously replied.

In the meantime, Boris and Irene had been patiently enjoying the little scene and were relishing this opportunity of being guests for a change. When asked, Boris would make a helpful suggestion.

As it turned out, the dinner was a gourmet's delight. There was little conversation as the group savored the delicious courses placed before them. They were sipping their brandy as George began to get impatient to go someplace where they could dance. He was very anxious to find out what kind of a dancer he had for a partner. Finally turning to his superior, he asked, "How about all of us going over to Chi Chi's? I have taken the liberty of reserving a table for tonight. Sir, I know Maria loves dancing with you. What do you think?"

The colonel's reaction was immediate. "I'm all for it. That's a good idea. Come on, let's drink up and we'll be on our way."

Freeburn finished his drink and rose from the table. Without noticing whether the others were ready to leave, he walked over behind Maria's chair and courteously helped her to her feet. As the two started for the door, the officer turned his head and impatiently asked, "Coming, Goerig?"

Tania was still sipping her brandy as George turned toward her and whispered, "He is my boss, you know. However, the sooner we get there, the more dancing we can get in."

His charming date laughed. "You are so smart, George. I love it."

With that, she leaned over and kissed him lightly on the cheek. Suddenly, the corporal gasped in astonishment as the top snap on her dress became undone and, unbelievingly, he found himself staring down at a bared, fully rounded breast with a tantalizing, pink nipple in full view. The girl was wearing no brassiere.

Quickly, Tania realized what had happened as she reached up for the errant strap. Embarrassed, she hastily glanced around. Fortunately, nobody had seemed to have noticed as she temporarily remedied the situation.

Gallantly, George leaned over and, kissing her tenderly on the cheek, softly murmured, "You are beautiful." The gesture was not very much appreciated at the time, but it did help ease the tenseness of what had happened.

With her tear-filled eyes and lips demurely quivering, she whispered aside, "George, that wasn't very proper of me. The next time, I will wear a brassiere."

Goerig politely ignored the temptation of telling her that she definitely did not need one. That would have been obvious, he figured. As the four rose to go, Tania discreetly asked Irene to go with her to the powder room. It was apparent that she did not want the same incident to occur again. George and Boris left to get the coats. They met the colonel in the lobby while he was making arrangements with the cashier for payment of the evening's festivities. The latter politely declined the offer from the two men to help pay their share of the cost of the dinner.

"This one is definitely on me," Freeburn firmly stated. "Maybe some other time, but not tonight."

Finally, they all got together and walked out into the cool evening. The cab driver was obediently waiting for them and bowed as he opened the door. Goerig climbed in first, indicating for Tania to follow him. The girl momentarily hesitated and then moved in to sit down on the corporal's lap.

"Now, isn't that nice, darling?" George asked. "And also, the colonel and Maria can be more comfortable this way."

Freeburn looked at his guest in a disapproving manner. Seeing that he had been outmaneuvered for the more intimate seat, he merely shrugged his shoulders and sarcastically answered, "Thanks George, it is nice of you to think of us."

As the cab moved cautiously out into the street, Tania warmly snuggled her tousled head conveniently on her escort's shoulder. "This is nice. *I like it," she she said, sighing contentedly.*

Goerig kissed her again lightly on the cheek and whisperingly sighed, "I love it."

He carefully and nonchalantly placed his free hand on the girl's firm tummy. As they road along and watched the flickering streetlights go by, the American decided to get friendlier. Moving his hand casually upward, he gently placed it over one of her rounded breasts and began to tenderly caress it. Just as nonchalantly, the Russian girl grasped the roving fingers and firmly placed them around her side in neutral territory. George was momentarily discouraged. He had lost the first round. However, he had gained some intimate knowledge about his partner's finer points. Time would tell.

The late evening crowd had filled most of the available tables at Chi Chi's. George was silently grateful he had had the foresight to make the necessary reservations beforehand. The orchestra had just finished playing a mixed medley of American songs as the group waited for the maître d.' George impatiently turned to Tania. and said, "Dammit, now we will have to wait awhile. I want to dance now."

"Now, darling," the girl purred as she disarmingly placed her arm around him in a consoling gesture. "There will be a lot more dances. We are going to have a lot of fun tonight. You just wait and see."

Her intimate use of the word "darling" momentarily surprised George and caused him to relax. As they followed the colonel over to their table, the corporal readily noticed that his elder superior was protectively holding Maria's arm and proudly showing off his young, beautiful date to the admiring patrons. George silently mused to himself, "Well, finally, it looks like I'm in like Flynn. And it only costs me a temporary girlfriend." Figuratively, he was right.

After a short respite, the orchestra returned to their seats. Goerig already had his date by her hand and was down on the dance floor before the first romantic strains of "Lullaby of the Leaves" reached their ears. As the two slowly moved into the swaying motions of the familiar tune, George happily realized that he had a perfect dancing partner by his side. Warmly, Tania glanced up at the man holding her in his arms and softly whispered, "You really do love to dance, don't you?"

Goerig, brushed her flushed cheek with his lips. "Dear, how right you are."

The lovely evening went by too fast. It was very apparent that the colonel was going to monopolize Maria's attention. George, in the meantime, wanted to spend a few moments with Irene. The opportunity arose when the other four excused themselves from the table. The blond Russian moved over next to the American soldier.

"Well, what do you think of Tania?"

"Dear, thanks a million. I think the doll is wonderful. I love your taste. It seems to me that everybody is happy and that's the way it should be. You are a perfect matchmaker, Irene, and a perfect hostess. If Boris doesn't mind, I'll say I love you for everything you have done."

She gratefully smiled and replied, "Boris is very thankful to you for what you have done for him. We both appreciate that. By the way, I see the men returning with our coats. I believe they are ready to leave. I do hope you two get along fine."

After stopping by Tania's apartment, George got out and escorted her over to the entrance. She was searching for the key in her purse when they heard an anxious voice calling, "Tania, is that you?"

"Yes, mother," was the reassuring reply. "I will be right up."

The corporal put his arms around the little Russian girl and held her close.

"Thanks for the wonderful evening. May I see you tomorrow night and the next and the next? I have some catching up to do."

Glancing up at George with her sparkling, dark eyes she whispered, "Anytime, I loved every minute of it." Then she paused and hesitantly reflected back on the one sorry embarrassing incident. "Well, almost every minute."

The two emotionally kissed as they swayed together. Finally, George released her and reluctantly opened the door. She lovingly glanced back upon entering. "Tomorrow night, then. Good night and thank you again."

Whistling lightly, George climbed in the front seat of the limousine next to the chauffeur and blithely ordered, "Home, James." After giving directions, the corporal welcomed the sight of his barracks. As he got out of the cab, his superior called to him. "See you tomorrow, George. I've got another project for you. Have a good sleep."

"Will do, sir. Good night and thanks for the lovely evening."

With a wave of his hand, he walked over to his building.

CHAPTER TWENTY-SEVEN

The following day was clear and brisk. Most of the autumn leaves had fallen from the scraggy trees, and the denuded branches were slowly moving back and forth like waving fingers in the soft breeze. It was a scene that made George feel quite sentimental and a bit homesick for his hometown in the States. It was Saturday, and he could envision the throngs of football fans back in Seattle preparing for their trek to the University of Washington stadium for the weekly football clash with one of their adversaries. He wishfully thought, "If I could only be there now."

The corporal was abruptly shaken out of his nostalgic reverie when he was approached by the first sergeant of their newly organized platoon. His name was Tony Newman, and he seemed to be one helluva a nice fellow.

"George, have you thought about applying for your transfer papers to get back to the States? A lot of the fellows are getting anxious to leave. I was wondering, with your set up here, if you were in a hurry or not."

Goerig exclaimed, "You damn right I'm in a hurry! Where do I sign?"

He got out of his jeep and followed the tall, blond, husky non-com over to the headquarters office. The non-com sat down at his desk and proceeded to explain the important point system that was involved in the determination of a man's eligibility to return Stateside. Goerig nodded.

"I know all about that, and I'm in the clear. Now where are the papers I sign?" the corporal impatiently asked.

As the sergeant placed the necessary documents in front of him, Goerig looked for the place to affix his signature. While doing so, Tony leaned over and casually asked, "By the way, when you leave Shanghai, do you think you might be able to fix me up for a date with that beautiful doll I've seen you out with lately? What's her name? Tania? She is one of the most attractive girls I have ever seen." He paused and then continued. "She seems to be a very nice person also. Not like those broads that hang around Chi Chi's."

George assuringly agreed that she was not like those "broads" in any way. In fact, he resented the idea of the sergeant including her in the same breath as those wanton whores.

"Tony, Tania is a very pretty and wonderful person. I like her very much. I'm flattered that you think about her in the same manner I do." George hesitated. "If you want to meet her, I'll be glad to introduce you. However, don't get any ideas of taking her out before I leave. I'm pretty jealous of her, even if she doesn't know it."

The big fellow nodded his head. "Don't worry, I'm getting along alright for the time being, and I doubt it would do me any good to even ask her out now. I've noticed the way she looks at you."

As George absentmindedly scanned over the papers before him, he was actually thinking about his relations with the Russian girl and how much he was going to miss her. However, since he was going, at least she would be left in proper hands. He didn't relish the idea of the word "hands," but what the hell could he do? He finally handed the papers back to the sergeant.

Tony began to explain. "The only Port of Debarkation now is Calcutta. I can get you lined up for there in a week or so. However, if you would rather take your chances, you can wait until the Fourteenth activates the Port of Shanghai as a returning area. What do you think?"

The private looked at him momentarily and mentally weighed the advantages of his choice of departure localities.

"Hell!" he finally exclaimed. "Why don't you send me to Calcutta? The flight down there won't take very long, and then I'm certain of getting home soon. You don't know when this area will be ready, and I'm ready now. I think a change of scenery might be good for me. I've had all the fun I want in Shanghai."

Tony smiled. "Suit yourself. I'll get the ball rolling."

George could picture what was going on in the non-com's mind and the future evenings the bastard was probably looking forward to with Tania in his arms. Goerig was tempted to say something, but he really didn't know what to say, except, "Well, thanks a lot. I've got to get back to the jobs."

Driving away in the jeep, he recalled the old saying, "Parting is such sweet sorrow." The phrase definitely seemed to fit the occasion of one private's coming departure from China.

The renovation and cleanup undertaken at the Sun Yat-sen Hospital was almost completed. Goerig had tripled the number of coolies he had started with and managed to select some capable sergeants from the Fourteenth to supervise the labor activities through the essential bilingual Chinese foremen.

The apartments at the University of Shanghai were rapidly being filled with Chinese professors, some of whom had been imprisoned during the war. Quite a few had been executed because of their failure to abide by the educational demands of the Japanese. However, the remainder provided a nucleus for a competent faculty. Upon moving back, they generally seemed quite pleased with their newly renovated and furnished suites.

Goerig had been a busy man. His efficient methods of planned organization and the expedient approach to the varied renovating problems before him were not going unnoticed by his superiors, although he had no stripes sewed on his sleeves as yet. In, fact not even pinned. Colonel Freeburn was pleasantly satisfied with his protege's accomplishments.

Personally, the corporal felt well rewarded for the periods of frustration he had endured under Captain Paine back on the Ledo Road. He thought that justice had finally prevailed, and he was content and very pleased with the situation.

The new project that his colonel had mentioned one day consisted of helping out with the improvement of the airfield lighting system around the runways at the airport outside of Shanghai. Not being an electrical expert, Goerig suggested to his superiors that it would be better if he could concentrate on the repair and resurfacing of the bombed areas the B-29s had cratered shortly prior to Hiroshima. The officer in charge was grateful for George's experience and ability to expedite this construction work.

It had been several days since he had seen Tania, and naturally George was anxious to take her out a few more times before he had to leave. Finally, he managed to contact her, and she told him she would love to go out. She knew of another cafe where the two of them could spend a quiet evening together. It was to be one evening that almost cost the American private his life.

Goerig had hired a pedicab for the evening. Since he had planned to spend the night at the hotel, he had left his jeep parked there so he could take off for work the first thing in the morning.

As George gazed at Tania over the candle lit table, he tried to express his true feelings, but he felt confused. How could he try and tell her he was sorry he was returning to the States and leaving her when he was actually eager to be going home?

The place was a secluded cafe with one violin player providing the music as he wandered among the tables. George was tired after the day's activities he suggested they leave fairly early. Tania reluctantly agreed.

At her doorstep, they kissed goodnight, and Goerig climbed back in the rented pedicab. He ordered the driver to take him downtown to the Parke Hotel where was looking forward to one more night at the fabulous hotel.

The private had briefly dozed off while he swayed to the steady rhythm of the cab's spoked wheels as it moved over the smooth paved surface of the main avenue. Suddenly, he became aware of an increased vibration, which caused him to open his eyes. The driver had swung off the thoroughfare and was heading down a cobblestone lane. George glanced at the unfamiliar buildings on each side of the poorly lit street.

The Chinese driver was busily hunched over his bike as Goerig reached in his pocket for the six-inch switchblade knife he always carried with him at night. Fully awake, he pressed the side button on the deadly weapon as it sprang open, presenting the shiny surface of the lethal blade. Without hesitation, the private leaped over the front of the cab and landed squarely on the back of the unsuspecting hi-jacker. The force of the momentum and the weight of his body caused them both to sprawl to the ground simultaneously. Roughly grabbing the would-be assassin by the shoulder, George twisted his fear-stricken face around till the coolie was wildly staring up at him. Placing the tip of the knife to his throat, Goerig pricked the taut skin and watched the blood begin to trickle down the side of his neck.

"You dirty rotten Chinese son of a bitch!" George yelled in uncontrolled rage. "You want to get me murdered? This isn't the way to the hotel. You get your gawd-damn ass up and turn this buggy around, then get me back on the avenue right now. *Quidi! Quidi!* Or I'll slit your fucking throat from ear to ear."

Goerig drew back the knife and angrily whacked the terrorized man a hard slap with the back of his hand. He then pulled him to his feet and dug the six-inch blade mercilessly into his back. George glanced nervously down the darkened street. It seemed to be deserted. However, within a block's distance, he could slightly discern several shadowy figures stealthily melting into the hidden sides of the adjacent buildings.

Shouting at the top of his lungs and shattering the stillness of the night, Goerig hysterically screamed shaking with rage, "Okay, you rotten bunch of bastards, here's one guy you didn't get for your stinking river!"

The pedicab was quickly turned around as Goerig walked beside the subdued driver. As they reached the main avenue, the private pointed his finger toward the downtown sector. Then with one final menacing swipe of his blade across the front of the man's neck, he climbed in and sat down. During the balance of the trip, Goerig remained constantly alert until they reached the entrance of the Parke Hotel.

Two uniformed policemen were standing at the side of the building. George got out and grabbed the shirt of the passive coolie and roughly dragged him across the sidewalk. He then angrily threw him at the feet of the startled officers.

With a feigned sweep of the knife across his throat, the private clearly indicated what the would-be assassin had attempted to do. Without need of further explanation, the two husky guards nodded and quickly began kicking the defenseless driver. Finally, they picked him up and pulled his arms up behind his back until the private clearly heard the snap of broken bones. Then they proceeded to haul the unfortunate prisoner down the street.

As George crossed the hotel lobby at the late hour, he approached the desk. The clerk on duty was a stranger. He asked the pleasant-faced man about Ashley, his good British friend. The American was informed that he had left for England a few weeks previously. After checking the requested reservation, the clerk looked up and smiled.

"Oh, you are Mister Goerig. I've heard a lot about you, especially from Johnnie, our new page master."

George quickly glanced up from the card in front of him and exclaimed, "Johnnie, a page master? How about that? He is moving up in the world. Kindly leave word for him that I'm back in the hotel for the night. When he comes on duty, please have him give me a call."

The corporal looked over at the tall clock standing against the wall with its long golden chimes. It was late and he mentally figured the few hours' sleep he would be able to get before dawn.

"Leave a call for me at seven," he told the man as he picked up his key and headed for the vacant elevator.

The clean, fresh sheets of the downy bed were inviting as George snuggled between then and reached over to turn out the light. He finally began to relax as his nerves, tense due to his near fatal-experience, began leaving his body.

"Thank God I'm still alive," he murmured and drowsily began to drift off into an intermittent sleep.

A cherry, welcoming, familiar voice was coming to him over the phone. "Mister Goerig, good morning. Time to get up. What will it be? Bloody Marys or wild cows?"

George shook his muddled head and hesitated before answering, "No, Johnnie, not this time. I have to go to work. Sorry, but I'll take a raincheck on it, though. Come on up and we'll have a short chat. Bring some orange juice and coffee."

"Coming right up, sir," Johnnie happily replied.

Reluctantly, the corporal climbed off the comfortable bed and headed for the bathroom. He looked at his face in the mirror. Noticing the five o'clock shadow, he swore, "Dammit, why didn't I tell him to bring up a razor and shaving cream? Oh, well, I'll shave when I get out at the base."

Following a brisk shower, he emerged with a large towel wrapped around his hips. Johnnie was just entering the door, carrying a welcome tray to the table in the middle of the room. On it was a razor and shaving cream. The loving little bastard always thought of everything. Well, not quite everything. George had slept alone last night, but of course his friend had not been on duty. Oh well, you can't win 'em all.

Johnnie proudly showed off his new stripes indicating his top rank as he knowingly glanced around the room.

"Not like your last suite, sir," Johnnie said, laughing.

Goerig walked over and clasped his hand warmly.

"Good to see you again, Johnnie. Come on over and sit down, we'll talk while I get dressed."

Picking up the glass of orange juice, he thirstily drank it down. His throat seemed unnaturally dry, and the cold liquid temporarily soothed his vocal chords. Gathering up his clothes, he began to get dressed.

"Well, what's been happening to you since I've been gone?" the corporal inquired.

"Not much, sir. The place has changed with all the new faces coming in. It's not like the old times when you were here, sir. We miss you."

George paused and looked over at the suddenly sad face. As he buttoned his khaki shirt, he reminisced, "Remember Maria? She is long gone out of my life. My colonel has taken her over, and they are both quite happy, I'm going with a now girl, Tania. I'll bring her down here some night before I go home, if I get the chance. You'll like her."

Johnnie rose quickly to his feet. "Going home?" he exclaimed. "So soon?"

Goerig's answer was very frank. "It's been too damn long as far as I'm concerned. I've got some wonderful people waiting for me back home, and I want to get my ass back there as soon as I can. Understand?"

The bellhop's expression changed and brightened at the prospects of his friend being back with his family again.

"I am glad for you, sir, and I sincerely hope everything works out fine. I am sorry to see you leave. I believe I had better go down and check on my boys. It has been really nice to see you again. Please write to me when you get home. I'd like to hear from you."

As Johnnie opened the door to leave, he turned and waved his hand. "Bon Voyage, as the French maid would say."

The American playfully threw a shoe at the boy as he disappeared though the doorway.

═

The following night, George and Tania were enjoying a tasty supper at her favorite cafe when she asked, "George, dear, for a change would you mind if we spent a quiet evening with my parents and grandparents at our apartment? I have told them so much about you, and they are anxious to sit and talk with you. I know you will find them interesting." She added, "Did you know that my grandfather was a duke in the royal court of Czar Nicholas, the Second, before the Revolution? He speaks very little English, but my parents are very proficient. I am sure you will love them."

Her obvious sincerity brought a quick reply.

"I'd love to, Tania. I am deeply interested in what happened to your family during and after the Revolution."

She was slowly sipping her Russian coffee, and a broad, thankful smile came over her tantalizing lips as her dark eyes sparkled. She laid down her cup and stood up. "Alright, I am ready. How about you?"

"Honey, I am always ready. Let's go."

═

George had briefly met the older generation of Tania's family. He was now looking forward to an enjoyable evening as he was intensely interested in the historical exodus of the white Russians before the cruel onslaught of the Red Army. From what he had heard, they were fortunate to reach the safety of Shanghai. It was the last leg of the journey from Harbin, Manchuria, an anticlimax to an unforgettable trap, that George was primarily interested in.

Their apartment was similar to Maria's. However, Goerig soon became oblivious to his surroundings as he became fascinated by the stories told by Tania's parents. Her grandparents were surprisingly alert, though the weathered lines of their drawn features reflected the hardships they must have endured over the past few decades.

They were all seated around a table in the center of the combined living and dining room as the girl's parents told the true story of the tragic incidences that occurred many years previously. George became entranced by the intriguing and fabulous stories of the royal court of Nicholas the Second. He listened intently to the tale of the tragic downfall of the monarchy at the hands of the brutal and communists under Vladimir Lenin. The evening proved to be a tremendous experience for the corporal from America, who had just happened to be born during the midst of the Red Revolution.

After several hours, Goerig finally found himself alone with Tania. Her folks had retired for the night, and he was unconsciously covering a yawn with his hand as he looked at his watch. It was 2:00 AM. He rose to go over and put on his jacket. A tired girl got up from her chair, put her arms around his neck, and kissed him tenderly on the lips.

"You are not going anywhere tonight," she firmly stated. "You are staying here with me."

Goerig was too tired to be surprised, though he did try to protest meekly. Tania put her hand over his mouth and said, "The streets are too dangerous at nighttime. It is not safe to be on them. You know what almost happened to you. My parents insisted that you sleep with me in my bed. So that is that."

George stepped back and stared at her disbelievingly.

"Well, that is a switch. I thought I was the one to do the seducing."

Tania's face became serious. "George, nobody is going to be seduced tonight, you will see." Then her expression changed, and she laughed. "Now, go in my bedroom and take off your clothes, except your underwear, and get into bed. I will be back shortly."

Goerig was in a daze as he walked into the bedroom. He was too astounded at the strange turn of events and too tired to argue. After he had closed the door and modestly turned out the lights, he obediently took off his clothes, leaving his underwear on. George then proceeded to slide in between the cool, fresh sheets. Suddenly his knee unexpectedly bumped into an object placed in the middle of the bed. He abruptly sat up and discovered that a wooden board had been placed down the center.

"Oh no," he murmured to himself. "Not all the way over here in China. Maybe New England in the olde days, but not in modern times."

He cautiously felt alongside of the ten-inch-high piece of lumber and decided he was definitely faced with a difficult barrier—temporarily, he hoped. No wonder her folks didn't mind his sleeping with their daughter. He also now understood Tania's indifference about his being her bed partner for the night.

George mumbled to himself, "I'll be damned if I am going to be so close and yet so far."

Finally, his demure little maiden, clad in a flowered modest nightgown, walked into the room and around to the other side of the bed. She climbed in, leaned over, and kissed her bedmate lightly on the check.

"Good night, George."

"Good night, dear," came the dejected answer.

George thought momentarily and then marveled at the ingenious but simple obstruction he was faced with. Then he turned over and strangely began dreaming about his forefathers and the tricks they must have used to overcome such situations. He was finding it hard to believe that such an outdated, frustrating device had been carried over into the twentieth century. Nobody did things like this anymore. At least, he hadn't heard of them.

It was a few hours later when George awoke and heard the soft steady breathing of his sleeping Cinderella beside him.

George thought slyly to himself, "You might as well try. What have you got to lose?"

Slowly, he had started to awkwardly climb over the wooden slat when he accidently bumped his knee. Unconsciously, he swore, "Dammit."

Tania sat up immediately and turning firmly but gently, pushed her ardent would-be lover back to his own side.

"Go to sleep, George. You'll, wake up the family."

Grudgingly, he moved back to his side of the bed and hopefully thought to himself, "Well, there goes the second round. I wonder if I'll get another chance?"

Eventually, sleep finally got the best of his amorous intentions as he realized that any further adventures had been cancelled for the night.

Chi Chi's, his old party time standby, was the scene of the private's final fling in Shanghai. He was not, however, quite prepared for the unexpected surprise, which came as a fitting climax to a wonderful evening.

Colonel Freeburn had been very busy in completing the final transition phases of the Fourteenth Engineer's move from Chungking to Shanghai. One afternoon, he called his favorite corporal into his office. Closing the door, he motioned for him to sit down at the side of his desk. The man seemed to be very preoccupied and concerned about what he was going to say.

"George, as you know, I've had the first sergeant working on your debarkation papers, since I know that you want to go home as soon as possible. I've made arrangements for you to fly to Calcutta within the week. Personally, I was hoping you would stick around until they open up Shanghai as a debarkation station. However, that is up to you. I just hope you don't get fouled up in Calcutta. It's not called the 'Black Hole of India' by the British for no reason at all."

He leaned back in his chair. "Anyway, let's change the subject. I would like to give a 'going away' party for you tonight, with Boris and Irene. How about it? Do you think Tania can make it?"

"Oh sir, that would be wonderful!" George exclaimed.

The colonel then lowered his voice and confidentially continued, "You know that I have been taking out Maria a few times lately."

Goerig considered that an understatement but remained discreetly silent.

His superior continued, "As farfetched as it may seem, I believe I have fallen seriously in love with the girl." He paused. "And I think she loves me. The only obstacle is that I am a married man with a daughter as old as Maria. However, living in Shanghai and going through what she has the past few years has made her into quite a mature person. Much more so than the average American girl her age. What do you think about the set up? Please let me know what you really think."

George was astounded by the sudden revelation he had just heard. At the same time, he felt good that the colonel trusted him so much as to bring him into his confidence regarding his personal affairs.

The private began, "Sir, I realize you have a problem. You've been away from home for quite a while. The situation that has suddenly arisen here in Shanghai is only natural. Maria is a very beautiful girl, and you are lonely for female companionship. When two people like you develop a fondness for each other, something is bound to happen. All I can suggest is that when you return Stateside, you discuss it with your wife. Who knows? She might have found someone else she likes while you've been gone."

Goerig suddenly thought about his wife, Helen, whom he hoped would still be waiting for him.

Freeburn firmly shook his head. "No, not Shirley. She is the true-blue type." Then he momentarily pondered. "Or is she? It's the first time I have ever been away for so long."

Since he felt he could offer no more suggestions, George figured it was time to go and leave the colonel reach his own conclusions. After all, he had plenty of worries on his own mind. How was he going to tell Tania he was a married man?

═

The evening started as most of their parties did, with cocktails at the Olienakov's apartment. It was from there to Chi Chi's, where a farewell party had been planned. The colonel appeared to be in a surprisingly genial mood, despite the personal problems he had discussed with George.

The group graciously exchanged dances at the night club. This gave George the opportunity to talk with Maria. As the two started to dance, the American smilingly looked down at the little Russian girl.

"Hi, dear, it's been a long time since we danced together. Did you miss me?"

She drew back her head, thinking her partner was serious. Then, seeing the grin on his face, she slowly replied, "Not much, George. As you know, I have been rather busy and, after all, you do have Tania. She is a good dancer."

Goerig's expression changed as he became serious.

"I know that," he answered "But, right now I am more interested in your affair with my colonel. Don't forget, I introduced you two and you have become quite a factor in his life. Has he talked to you about how much you mean to him?"

Maria moved closer and whispered, "Yes, he has. What is worse is that I think I have fallen in love with him. I shouldn't have, because I know he is a married man and I know better, or at least I should. It is a wrong thing to do, but I couldn't help myself. He is a lot older, though he is so sweet and nice to me, I just love him."

The final strains of the waltz were dying away, and the couple started back to the table as George leaned over and murmured in the girl's ear, "Please don't worry. Everything will work out alright for both of you."

═

George and Tania stopped in front of her apartment as he put his arms tenderly around the sad-eyed doll, and held her close to him. He whispered in her ear, "I'm going to really miss you."

She turned her head and kissed him lightly on the cheek.

"I am going to miss you, terribly, George. I think I have fallen in love with you. I didn't want to, because I know that you will have to leave soon and go back to your wife and children."

Goerig drew back and his mouth started to fall open. "Wife and children? You've known all this time that I am married, and you didn't let on?"

"Irene told me all about it the first night we went out. She did not want to see me get hurt. That is the reason I have never let you make love to me." She hesitated. "It was not that I didn't want to. Every time you held me in your arms, I felt so close to you, and I really wanted all of you. But that is not good. Now you know. I do love you."

She fumbled in her purse and brought out a handkerchief. Suddenly, she burst into tears and threw her arms around him. Sobbingly, she cried in his ear.

"Oh George, why does it have to be this way? I do love you and I am going to miss you."

Then, stepping back, Tania began wiping the tears from her eyes.

"Please write to me when you get home. I would like to hear from you. Now, I must go in."

George reached for her and gently lifted her chin. He traced the quivering lips with his finger.

"Tania, I do love you. I will remember you always. Let's just be happy that we had such wonderful times together. I will miss you." He took her by the arm. "It's best that you go in now, before I get too sentimental and break down."

They slowly walked over to the door, and she unlocked it. Turning, the girl briefly kissed George on the cheek and said, "Goodbye, darling. Thank you again for everything. Please take care of yourself."

She closed the door softly, and he could hear the muffled sound of her steps going up the stairway. Walking over to the jeep, Goerig climbed in and turned on the ignition. “Dammit,” he swore.

CHAPTER TWENTY-EIGHT

George was stowing his gear in the barracks bag and discarding a few items that he had no use for on his trip back home. The extra space that had previously been filled with Chinese Nationalist Notes was sadly depleted. He used that to send a few extra souvenirs he had failed to mail Stateside. The private had managed to spend a major portion of the loot and had had the balance changed into an American mail order, which he sent to Helen, his wife.

He had left her with substantial money in the bank previous to going overseas, which, in addition to his dependent's allotment, had provided her with sufficient funds to get by on. His brother, in Seattle, also lent a hand when she needed it. Goerig wondered what kind of shape the fairly new car was in that he had left her. Oh well, he could worry about that later.

As he was placing the last of his toiletry articles on top of his clothing, a loud announcement came over the speaker system.

"Attention! Everybody out on the double. Line up in front of headquarters."

The private muttered to himself, "What the hell is going on now?"

Most of all the Army formalities had all but been forgotten, and even some of the traditional military rituals were being by-passed in favor of more important things. A motley crew dressed in all descriptions of attire stood at ease before the first sergeant, and George dutifully joined the waiting group as Colonel Freeburn strode out from this office.

"Atten-shun!" barked the sergeant.

"At ease," began their superior. "I just want to present a medal to one of you. It seems that he is leaving today to go home." He smiled. "Don't we all wish we were that lucky?"

A few knowing, envious looks were cast in Goerig's direction.

"Corporal Goerig, front and center," Freeburn ordered.

The man standing behind the new corporal gave him a push. "That's you, Goerig."

He hesitated, then briskly walked over in front of the colonel and smartly saluted. The officer opened a small box he held in his hand.

"Corporal Goerig, the Fourteenth Air Force is proud to present you with this token of their appreciation, the Bronze Star Medal, for meritorious service while serving as a private in Laifeng, China. Congratulations, George."

He then stepped forward and pinned the shiny, golden medal on Goerig's khaki shirt. They exchanged salutes. Freeburn smiled and said, "Good luck, Corporal."

Goerig choked. "Thank you, sir. It means a lot to me."

The formation was dismissed.

The trip to Calcutta was an anticlimax after Goerig's stay in China. As he sat in the bucket seat of the C-47, he gazed at the green landscape far below with its multitude of rice paddies dominating the countryside. The steady hum of the straining engines gave him a confident feeling. He was finally going home. Looking around at the interior of the plane, he noticed it was filled with other GIs in the same situation. Most of the men seemed to be daydreaming, perhaps about a reunion with their loved ones. Others were excitedly talking about the first things they were going to do when they finally reached home. It was a very happy group.

The stop at Chungking was a short one. In the few hours that George was there, he learned that most of the engineers, including Bob and Dale, had left for home via the air route he was taking through Calcutta. Some of the men, however, had taken the opportunity to go to Shanghai and try their chances of leaving from there. They were also interested in visiting the famed "Paris of the East."

Goerig momentarily wondered whether he had made a mistake in choosing Calcutta as his port of debarkation. He soon found out his choice had indeed been quite a mistake.

While at the Chungking airbase, the corporal had tried to contact Suzy, but to no avail. He felt lonely and disappointed that he wouldn't be able to talk with her once more.

After a short layover and a quick meal, the group boarded their plane again. This time for Kunming.

The transition of that huge base had practically been completed. The comparative calmness and serenity of the area seemed to be in sharp contrast to the scene of organized confusion that had prevailed upon his first arrival in that sector of the CBI theater.

Their final flight over the Himalayas, more commonly known as the Hump, was still breathtaking. The snow-covered mountains were awe inspiring in their majestic splendor. Despite the fact that he was finally on his way home, Goerig realized that his recent adventures and the vast area of country he had visited would always be an unforgettable experience.

Parsing over the sprawling city of Calcutta, George was amazed at the density of the Indian metropolis. Shortly, the transport landed at Barrachpore airbase. From there it was a short ride to Camp Kanchrapara, a replacement depot that served as a staging camp for GIs returning home from China.

It was in the middle of November when the corporal moved to Camp Angus about twenty miles distance from the big city, or so-called Black Hole of India. The accommodations were far superior to the miserable facilities at his last resting place. However, Goerig was getting increasingly impatient to board his home-bound transport. He continually visited the camp headquarters to try and learn when he was going to be able to leave that God-forsaken country. He was beginning to believe that Colonel

Freeburn had been right in suggesting that he disembark from Shanghai. It was then that an incredible incident occurred.

"Hey, Goerig, what the hell are you doing here?" someone yelled.

Looking ahead about thirty feet, the corporal stopped in amazement. It was Captain McEvoy, the medical officer from his old engineering battalion on the Ledo Road. He could hardly believe his eyes as he rushed forward and warmly clasped the doctor's hand. Being so taken by the unexpected meeting with his former neighbor from the lakeside apartments, George hardly noticed the two officers standing by and obviously enjoying the sight of the happy reunion.

"By the way, George, I believe you already know Captain Paine and Lieutenant Faults." McEvoy nodded his head in the direction of his two companions. The corporal paused as he stared at his former superior and adversary, who had vainly tried to have him court martialed.

Paine extended his hand. Goerig hesitantly shook it while at the same time noticing the colored ribbon of the Bronze Star Medal on his shirt. George couldn't help but chuckle as he pointed to the duplicate he was wearing, stating, "I guess the Army must have a surplus of those things. It looks like they give them away to anybody."

The four men laughed at the coincidence as the past animosity suddenly seemed to disappear. As they talked, it was apparent they were all in the same predicament regarding their futile efforts to find out when the group would be leaving.

Finally, as George shook hands with his doctor friend, they both vowed they would meet again back in their home town of Seattle. The captain suggested that the cocktail bar at the College Club would be a convenient and appropriate place for the reunion. Goerig heartily agreed.

Leaving the surprised trio, the corporal silently recalled his unfortunate experiences in Burma. He shuddered as he realized how very close he had been to having his Army career terminated with a tragic ending. Instead, due to the unexpected intervention of one interested person in Calcutta and the special request from General Chenault, George had experienced one of the greatest individual exploits of a peaceful nature in the annals of the CBI theater of war. He should have been extremely thankful to Captain Paine for his unintentional aid in helping him achieve his goal.

Everything now seemed to be anti-climax as the corporal waited impatiently for news of his future travel orders. During this period, however, he had occasion to visit the city of Calcutta. While there, he accepted an invitation to join a Red Cross tour of the steaming metropolis.

Calcutta, the second largest city in the British Empire, with a population of over two million, was a mixture of nationalities as varied as there were countries to come from. In the modern sections, the architecture was of the latest design. The streets were well paved and the residences were of the highest quality. However, in the outlying districts, the hovels were nothing but slums of the lowest standard. On all sides, humanity in all its splendor and abject poverty existed everywhere. Professional beggars, bankers, merchants, cripples, and religious fanatics mingled to make Calcutta one of the world's most intriguing, mysterious cities.

Nowhere in the world was there a greater potpourri of religion than in India. Many impressive temples had been erected there, chief among which were the dazzling, ornate Jain temple, the Kali temple, the Sikh temples, and the Moslem mosques.

Sacred cattle roamed freely on the city's proud boulevards. The new and old clashed as bullock carts vied with double-decker buses. It was not uncommon to witness smoke rising from burning ghats as dead bodies were cremated in open squares until only ashes remained.

The weeks passed by slowly until George finally received his orders and proceeded to board the long-awaited transport with hundreds of other hopeful civilians bound for the States. Grown men, not boys anymore. As he struggled up the gangplank, Goerig hesitated and wistfully looked back at the country he had once dreamed of visiting. Those dreams had been fulfilled in a most unorthodox fashion, as his experiences had far exceeded his most imaginative visions. But was he ever happy about going home? You damn right he was!

The following day, after high tide, the ship slowly moved out into the current of the Hooghly River, and with bow anchor dragging, they dropped downstream only to anchor again a few miles from Calcutta. On the next tide, they proceeded still farther but again anchored to wait out an ebb tide. In the early evening, the ship finally bore the excited but tired passengers into the open sea.

Now on his own, the Corporal was responsible directly to no one. He managed to escape the duties of any details, which included KP. Kitchen patrol had been placed on a rotating basis. Surprisingly, numerous "chow hounds" repeatedly volunteered for the previously hated assignment. The food was excellent in comparison to the last fare Goerig had had in India. The unlimited quantities of cold milk and ice cream were in great demand from the hungry troops. The wonderful food, coupled with the realization that they were going home, kept morale on a high plane.

As they neared the Philippines, the corporal wondered whether or not his brother-in-law, Arnie West, was still stationed there. When the transport unexpectedly dropped anchor in the Port of Manila, the men were mildly surprised to see a small harbor boat come alongside with an escort of arm-banded military police. The MPs boarded the ship and quickly left with an enlisted female of the Women's Auxiliary Corps in tow. It was shortly after the boarding by the MPs and as the transport was cutting its way through the blue waters of the Pacific Ocean that the scuttlebutt was out that the woman had invaded the privacy of the captain's quarters. Whether she was sexually too impatient to wait till she reached the States, or whether she just wanted to make nautical history with the captain, will remain a mystery.

It seems that when the ship's commanding officer returned to his stateroom from the bridge, he found a very naked girl partaking of his stock of assorted liquors. Being the strait, or rather stupid, sailor that he was, the officer had ordered the female intruder to be taken off the ship at the nearest port. It seemed like a crazy idea when there was over a thousand sex-hungry men on board who would have been more than happy to please the unfortunate girl. Oh well, to each his own.

Goerig's odyssey reached a climax as the *Victory* decked at Tacoma, Washington, a short thirty miles from home. Peering over the rail, George spotted his brother among the noisy throng on the dock. He was waving one arm, and with the other, he raised up a welcoming bottle of booze. He hadn't forgotten after all.

Hurriedly sliding down the steep, unfamiliar steps from the upper deck, George suddenly slipped and fell at the bottom rungs as his momentum carried him into a steel railing. As he picked himself up, he felt the bridge of his nose. Withdrawing his hand, he noticed no trace of blood. Triumphantly, he laughed. After twenty-seven months, Corporal Goerig had finally become a war casualty. His trip had not been in vain.

"Thank you, General Chenault, for your unforgettable RSVP."

VOL A 187 PAGE 162

HONORABLE DISCHARGE

G

1. LAST NAME - FIRST NAME - MIDDLE INITIAL	2. ARMY SERIAL NO.	3. GRADE	4. ARM OR SERVICE	5. COMPONENT
GOERIG GEORGE E SR	39 212 913	SGT	AAF	AUS

6. ORGANIZATION	7. DATE OF SEPARATION	8. PLACE OF SEPARATION
14TH AAF ENG COMMAND	30 DEC 45	SEPARATION CENTER FORT LEWIS WASH

9. PERMANENT ADDRESS FOR MAILING PURPOSES	10. DATE OF BIRTH	11. PLACE OF BIRTH
SPOKANE COUNTY 2812 W BROAD ST SPOKANE WASH	10 MAR 17	SEATTLE WASH

12. ADDRESS FROM WHICH EMPLOYMENT WILL BE SOUGHT	13. COLOR EYES	14. COLOR HAIR	15. HEIGHT	16. WEIGHT	17. NO. DEPEND.
SEE 9	BROWN	BROWN	5-9	155 LBS.	3

18. RACE: WHITE	NEGRO	OTHER (specify)	19. MARITAL STATUS: SINGLE	MARRIED	OTHER (specify)	20. U.S. CITIZEN: YES	NO	21. CIVILIAN OCCUPATION AND NO.
X				X		X		CONSTRUCTION FOREMAN 5-94.000

MILITARY HISTORY

22. DATE OF INDUCTION	23. DATE OF ENLISTMENT	24. DATE OF ENTRY INTO ACTIVE SERVICE	25. PLACE OF ENTRY INTO SERVICE
9 AUG 43		30 AUG 43	FT LEWIS WASH

SELECTIVE SERVICE DATA — 26. REGISTERED: YES	NO	27. LOCAL S.S. BOARD NO.	28. COUNTY AND STATE	29. HOME ADDRESS AT TIME OF ENTRY INTO SERVICE
X		7	SEATTLE WASH	1515 E THOMAS SEATTLE WASH

30. MILITARY OCCUPATIONAL SPECIALTY AND NO.	31. MILITARY QUALIFICATION AND DATE (i.e., infantry, aviation and marksmanship badges, etc.)
CONSTRUCTION FOREMAN 059	MARKSMAN M1 RIFLE & CARBINE

32. BATTLES AND CAMPAIGNS

BURMA CHINA

33. DECORATIONS AND CITATIONS BRONZE STAR MEDAL GO 9 HQ 14 AF '45
EUROPEAN AFRICAN MIDDLE EASTERN SERVICE MEDAL VICTORY MEDAL
ASIATIC-PACIFIC SERVICE MEDAL GOOD CONDUCT MEDAL VICTORY MEDAL

34. WOUNDS RECEIVED IN ACTION

NONE

35. LATEST IMMUNIZATION DATES: SMALLPOX	TYPHOID	TETANUS	OTHER (specify)
APR 45	NOV 44	DEC 43	AUG 45 TYPH

36. SERVICE OUTSIDE CONTINENTAL U.S. AND RETURN: DATE OF DEPARTURE	DESTINATION	DATE OF ARRIVAL
24 MAR 44	AP	11 MAY 44
21 NOV 45	US	24 DEC 45

37. TOTAL LENGTH OF SERVICE — CONTINENTAL SERVICE: YEARS	MONTHS	DAYS	FOREIGN SERVICE: YEARS	MONTHS	DAYS	38. HIGHEST GRADE HELD
0	6	29	1	9	1	SGT

39. PRIOR SERVICE

NONE

40. REASON AND AUTHORITY FOR SEPARATION

CONVENIENCE OF GOVERNMENT RR1-1 "DEMOBILIZATION" AR 615-365 15 DEC 44

41. SERVICE SCHOOLS ATTENDED	42. EDUCATION (Years): Grammar	High School	College
NONE	8	4	4

PAY DATA

43. LONGEVITY FOR PAY PURPOSES: YEARS	MONTHS	DAYS	44. MUSTERING OUT PAY: TOTAL	THIS PAYMENT	45. SOLDIER DEPOSITS	46. TRAVEL PAY	47. TOTAL AMOUNT, NAME OF DISBURSING OFFICER
2	4	21	$ 300	$ 100	None	$ 2.80	290.24 WALTER S BURK MAJOR FD

INSURANCE NOTICE

IMPORTANT IF PREMIUM IS NOT PAID WHEN DUE OR WITHIN THIRTY-ONE DAYS THEREAFTER, INSURANCE WILL LAPSE. MAKE CHECKS OR MONEY ORDERS PAYABLE TO THE TREASURER OF THE U. S. AND FORWARD TO COLLECTIONS SUBDIVISION, VETERANS ADMINISTRATION, WASHINGTON 25, D. C.

48. KIND OF INSURANCE: Nat. Serv.	U.S. Govt.	None	49. HOW PAID: Allotment	Direct to V. A.	50. Effective Date of Allotment Discontinuance	51. Date of Next Premium Due (One month after 50)	52. PREMIUM DUE EACH MONTH	53. INTENTION OF VETERAN TO: Continue	Continue Only $	Discontinue
X			X		31 DEC 45	31 JAN 46	$ 6.80	X		

54. RIGHT THUMB PRINT

55. REMARKS (This space for completion of above items or entry of other items specified in W. D. Directives)

LAPEL BUTTON ISSUED

ASR SCORE (2 SEP 45) 81

INACTIVE SERVICE ERC FROM 9 AUG 43 TO 30 AUG 43

56. SIGNATURE OF PERSON BEING SEPARATED	57. PERSONNEL OFFICER (Type name, grade and organization - signature)
George E Goerig Sr.	ALVIN B YODER MAJOR CAVALRY

WD AGO FORM 53-55
1 November 1944

This form supersedes all previous editions of WD AGO Forms 53 and 55 for enlisted persons entitled to an Honorable Discharge, which will not be used after receipt of this revision.

FILED for Record at Request of

www.ingramcontent.com/pod-product-compliance
Lightning Source LLC
LaVergne TN
LVHW041200150826
845673LV00001B/235

* 9 7 9 8 9 8 8 0 4 0 8 4 2 *